WITHDRAWN

The nineteenth century in Britain is often known as the Victorian Age. For many years, "Victorian" was a term of abuse; now, we are better able to see what was good in this remarkable period during which our modern way of life was shaped. Victoria's reign (1837–1901) was an age of invention, of discovery, of heroism, of confidence in an endless progress towards a better way of life. Above all it was an age of contradictions—of huge wealth and desperate poverty, of saintly charity and devilish meanness, of new ideas and fanatical prejudice.

What was she like, this tiny woman who ruled for sixty-four years over the world's most powerful nation, who gave her name to everything from railway stations to an Australian state? Queen Victoria too was a mass of contradictions – she was thoroughly happy to be a woman monarch, but she thought it disgusting that women should dream of becoming doctors. She was less than five feet tall, and neither beautiful nor regal in appearance. Yet she was loved by her people as few rulers have ever been loved, and statesmen from Europe to India trembled when the "Great White Queen" showed her displeasure.

Richard Garrett's *Queen Victoria* is a fascinating portrait of the woman and the sovereign. It reveals her thoughts on public and private affairs during twenty years of idyllic love with Prince Albert, and forty years of unhappy widowhood. It also shows how she helped to shape the world in which we live today.

WAYLAND KINGS AND QUEENS

Queen Victoria

Richard Garrett

WAYLAND PUBLISHERS LONDON

Kings and Queens Series

Alfred the Great Jennifer Westwood
Henry VIII David Fletcher
Mary Queen of Scots Alan Bold
Elizabeth I Alan Kendall
James I David Walters
Charles I Hugh Purcell
Charles II Michael Gibson
Louis XIV Christopher Martin
Napoleon Stephen Pratt
Charlemange Keith Ellis
Charles V William Raine
Kaiser Bill Richard Garrett
Peter the Great Michael Gibson
Catherine the Great Miriam Kochan
George III Amanda Purves

History Makers Series

The Last Czar W. H. C. Smith
Hitler Matthew Holden
Goering F. H. Gregory
Lenin Lionel Kochan
Karl Marx Caroline Seaward
The Wright Brothers Russell Ash
Cecil Rhodes Neil Bates
Picasso David Sweetman
Al Capone Mary Letts
Stalin F. H. Gregory and David Hayes
Captain Scott David Sweetman
Jomo Kenyatta Julian Friedmann
The Borgias David Sweetman
Martin Luther King Patricia Baker
Bismarck Richard Kisch
Rommel F. H. Gregory
Franco Richard Kisch
Mao Tse-tung Hugh Purcell

82-812 8/6-82 Mainline 9.95

Frontispiece Victoria with her dog Sharp at Balmoral in 1867. This is one of the very few portraits that shows her smiling.

SBN 85340 387 2
Copyright © 1974 by Wayland (Publishers) Ltd.
First published in 1974 by
Wayland (Publishers) Ltd.
49 Lansdowne Place, Hove, East Sussex, BN3 1HF
2nd impression 1977
3rd impression 1978
Printed in Great Britain by Butler & Tanner Ltd.
Frome and London

Contents

1 The Birth of a Queen

IN THE EARLY SPRING OF 1819, citizens on the road from western Germany to the French coast watched with interest as a large, antiquated coach rattled by. A royal Duke, muttering angrily about the rutted highway, sat at the reins. The roof and the interior of the vehicle were crammed with servants, pets and baggage. In one corner, a short, plump little woman sat propped up against the cushions. She had pink cheeks, and her brown hair was surprisingly well groomed. She seemed to be enduring the discomforts of the trip bravely, but she and her husband, the Duke, were worried. As her figure made clear, she was eight months pregnant. Heaven knew what damage this incessant bumping and jolting might be doing. They both prayed silently that they would reach London in time for their baby's arrival.

It would have been more prudent if the Duke of Kent, for he was the royal driver, had arranged the journey earlier, but this had been impossible. He had been suffering from one of his many financial crises. Only at the last moment had this father-to-be managed to raise enough cash for his small expedition; even then, he could not afford a coachman.

Behind them lay the small town of Amorsbach. It was there that the baby had been conceived, but the Duke was determined that his child should be born in London. He was, after all, fourth in line to the throne of Britain. Had he been honest, he might have added that he was also a very superstitious man. A gipsy on the island of Malta had once told him that he would become the father of a great queen. At the time, it had been an

Opposite Princess Victoria, aged two, with her mother the Duchess of Kent.

Above Queen Victoria's father, the Duke of Kent.

unlikely prophecy, but he had believed her. Only London – and, to be more specific, Kensington Palace – would be a suitable birthplace for a Queen of England.

The Duke urged the reluctant horses on. For seven horrible days, and for seven scarcely less uncomfortable nights, when, to save money, they stayed at cheap inns, the coach lurched on its way westwards. When, at last, they reached the Channel, a gale was blowing. The crossing was even worse than the ordeal by land. But the Duchess held on to her baby, and the Duke fretfully searched the horizon for a first glimpse of England.

At last the awful journey was over. On the 24th April, the battered and filthy coach, with its royal couple, its trunk and its retinue of servants, and its other living cargo of canaries and dogs, arrived at Kensington Palace. Just over three weeks later, on 19th May, the Duchess gave birth to a baby girl. After a great deal of discussion, she was baptized Alexandrina Victoria.

The Maltese gipsy had made a bold prophecy when she predicted that the Duke of Kent would father a sovereign. His father, King George III, was still on the throne. There were three brothers older than himself, each of whom might produce an eligible child. Only the Prince Regent (later George IV) obliged. In 1796, his wife gave birth to Charlotte, Princess of Wales. Charlotte was eventually betrothed to Prince Leopold of Saxe-Coburg-Saafield. Provided they had a child, the royal succession was assured.

On the morning of 6th November, 1817, Princess Charlotte went into labour. Some hours later, she died and the baby who might have become King of England was stillborn. By this time, it seemed unlikely that any of the elder Princes, who were now middle-aged, would beget an heir. The House of Hanover began to tremble. Members of Parliament panicked, knowing that the country might be plunged into chaos if the succession was disputed. Presently people began to look hopefully at the Duke of Kent as if he were the prime exhibit in a bloodstock show. Perhaps the words of the Maltese seer might come true after all.

"My master is the best of all husbands in all the five corners of the globe; and his wife bears him an amount of love, the greatness of which can only be compared with the English national debt." *Christian Stockmar on the marriage of Prince Leopold to Princess Charlotte*

Edward Augustus, Duke of Kent, was already fifty-two years old. He had enjoyed a fairly successful military career, and had reached the rank of Field Marshal. In 1802, he had been appointed Governor General of Gibraltar, but he held the post for only one year. At the end of it, he was dismissed on charges of brutality. The accusations seemed most out of character; for this large, stout man, with his thick black eyebrows and his carefully dyed hair, was not an unkindly individual. He was strict with his men, and some described him as a martinet. Nevertheless, he was one of the first to propose an end to flogging in the army. So far as he had any political views at all, he believed in a rather impractical form of socialism. His hobbies were designing clocks and striving to create some sort of order out of his invariably chaotic financial affairs.

The Duke had been living happily with a lady named Julie de St. Laurent. The arrangement had suited him admirably, but it could not solve the present crisis. Mlle de St. Laurent (even if he agreed to marry her) was a commoner. To produce an heir to the throne, the Duke would have to marry a woman of royal blood.

One might think that the Duke of Kent agreed to abandon Mlle de St. Laurent, and seek out a more suitable wife, for reasons of patriotic duty. This may, indeed, have been among his motives, but the real reason seems to have been money. When his brother the Duke of York had married, Parliament had voted him an annual allowance of £25,000. Might he not expect a similar reward? Could this be the end of his struggles to make ends meet?

He proposed (successfully) to Victoria of Saxe-Coburg, the widow of a German princeling and the sister of Leopold, whose wife, Charlotte, had died on that dark November day in 1817. As things turned out, however, he was disappointed in his financial expectations. Parliament was in a meaner mood this time. His annuity was increased by a paltry £6,000 a year – which, as the Duke was the first to point out, was nothing like enough. However, there was remarkably little he

Above Queen Victoria's mother, the Duchess of Kent.

"They are the damnedest millstones about the necks of any Government that can be imagined. They have insulted – *personally* insulted – two-thirds of the gentlemen of England, and how can it be wondered that they take their revenge upon them in the House of Commons?"
Duke of Wellington on the Duke of Kent and his brother, the Duke of Clarence

could do about it.

The couple began their married life in Brussels, and later moved to Amorsbach in Germany. When, a few months later, they came to England, it was still not certain that their child would succeed to the throne, for the Duke of Clarence (later William IV) had unexpectedly become a father. Two months before Victoria's birth, his wife had presented him with a small girl, who died almost at once. In 1821, she produced another daughter, who struggled through three sickly months of life before dying too. The way to the crown was now clear.

By this time, however, the Duke was in no position to worry about it. Shortly after Victoria's birth, the family moved down to the coast at Sidmouth, thinking that the sea air would do her good. On some excursion or other, the Duke got his feet wet. A chill developed into pneumonia. He died in 1820, leaving the Duchess virtually penniless, with few friends at court and her brother Leopold as the only source of advice and financial help.

The Duchess returned with her baby to London and the shelter of Kensington Palace. The story of Victoria's ascent to the throne had begun.

Below Kensington Palace, Victoria's birthplace, drawn in 1831.

2 The Days of Childhood

THE YOUNG PRINCESS VICTORIA was a podgy infant, with fair hair and blue eyes. As she grew older, she was given to tantrums, and one of her governesses said she had never seen "such a naughty child." Nevertheless, she was, they all agreed, very pretty, and she had one great virtue. She always spoke the truth. For the first three years of her life, she spoke it in German, for this was the only language she heard.

She lived with her mother, and Uncle Leopold was a constant caller. There were visits from her German grandmother (who called her "May Blossom," and contentedly observed that "the English like Queens"). She began to study English shortly after her third birthday, and her quick ear enabled her to pick up the language quickly. Many years later, her eldest son (Edward VII) was a constant reminder of his German ancestors, for he always spoke with a thick accent. Victoria's pronounciation was faultless: pure, melodious, and regal.

Her mother, the Duchess of Kent, may have looked outwardly like a plump and amiable German housewife. Inside, however, she was a powerhouse of ambition. Her royal brothers-in-law had done little to disguise their dislike for her, no doubt because she and her husband had succeeded in having a child where they had failed. When George III died at last in 1820, having been almost insane for the last twenty years of his life, the newly crowned George IV refused to have anything to do with her. Debauched and ageing, he lurked in sulky silence at Windsor. Leopold was her

"The general bent of her character is strength of intellect, capable of receiving with ease, information, and with a peculiar readiness in coming to a very just and benignant decision on any point her opinion is asked on. Her adherance to the truth is of so marked a character that I feel no apprehension of that Bulwark being broken down under any circumstances." *The Duchess of Kent on Victoria as a young girl*

Below A sketch made by Victoria herself of Baroness Lehzen, her governess.

only friend, and whatever advice he gave usually stemmed from a highly intelligent German doctor named Christian Stockmar.

Stockmar's father had been an unimportant magistrate in the German town of Coburg. After training as a doctor, the young man served as a medical officer in the army. Later he met Prince Leopold, who offered him a post as his personal physician. But Christian Stockmar's medical ability was nothing when set beside his talent for diplomacy. He became Leopold's trusted friend, and the Prince seldom did anything without seeking his opinion. When Leopold was offered the throne of Greece, it was Stockmar who advised him to refuse it. And when, in 1830, Belgium cut itself off from Holland, and Leopold was invited to become the fledgling nation's first monarch, it was Stockmar who told him to accept.

No doubt the Duchess of Kent was grateful for the guidance of this great soothsayer, for she was now an intrepid traveller through the jungle of monarchy. She was determined that Victoria should not only come to the throne, but that she should be suitably prepared for queenship.

The Duchess was strong-willed and possessive, and insisted that her daughter should be exposed only to the right influences. At night, the youngster had to sleep in mama's bedroom: during the daytime, she was never left alone for one minute. Somebody had to supervise her education, and it was Stockmar the infallible who hit upon the happy idea of engaging a clergyman's daughter from Hanover. Her name was Louise Lehzen.

A lady-in-waiting named the Baroness de Späth had taught Victoria to make pretty cardboard boxes by decorating them with tinsel and painted flowers. Her mother was looking after her religious instruction, and she did it wholeheartedly. At the age of six, the unfortunate Victoria was made to sit through tedious sermons in church on Sunday mornings. In the afternoon, she was questioned on them in detail. It may have been a healthy reaction against the antics of the royal uncles, who were still following their wayward path of drinking, gambling and womanizing. Even so, it is impossible not to marvel at the young Princess's patience on these occasions.

It must have been hard, for patience was not her strongest characteristic. When Fraulein Lehzen arrived from Germany, she summed up the five-year old child with penetrating accuracy. This job was going to need firmness – there was no doubt about it. But firmness, on its own, would not be enough. It would also need affection. If she could not become fond of Victoria, and if Victoria did not like her, she might as well pack her trunk again, and go home to the parsonage at Hanover.

With lesser governesses to assist her, she succeeded magnificently. She helped her charge to dress a collection of 132 wooden dolls. She taught her history, and even read it aloud when the young Princess was being dressed. Above all things, she encouraged Victoria to keep a dairy – a habit which lasted throughout her life.

For the young girl, who had never known a father and who was dominated by an ambitious mother, it was a strangely lonely life. One of her few playmates was the daughter of her mother's major-domo, or head of the household, Sir John Conroy; but there was always a red-coated footman present on these occasions. Victoria was never allowed to forget her position. As she told another little girl, "You must not touch those, they are mine; and I may call you Jane, but you must not call me Victoria."

Westcliffe House, Ramsgate, where the Duchess of Kent and the young Victoria spent seaside holidays.

Into this bleak and highborn atmosphere, Fraulein Lehzen brought comfort and understanding. No doubt the Duchess loved her daughter, but it was a jealous and scheming brand of affection. Had she looked at things with more understanding, she might have realized that her position as a mother was gradually being taken over by the affectionate governess.

At last George IV relented in his attitude to the Duchess and to Victoria, and the little girl was invited to the Royal Lodge at Windsor. The King asked the Princess to "give me your little paw," and invited her to kiss the heavily rouged royal cheek. On the following day, he took her to Virginia Water, where the members of his court were fishing from a large boat. A band was playing. "What is your favourite tune?" he asked his small guest. "The band shall play it." With a tact which seems almost too good to be true, Victoria replied, "God Save the King, Sir."

When she went home, she had reasonably happy memories of the man she referred to as "Uncle King."

But Uncle King was not to rule for much longer. He died in 1830, and was succeeded by his brother William IV. William shared his dislike of the Duchess of Kent. He was uncomfortably aware that, if he, too, died before Victoria was of age, his scheming sister-in-law would become Regent. Indeed, it is said that he prayed earnestly to be allowed to cling on to life until Victoria was twenty-one. He cannot have prayed hard enough; for he died in 1837, when his successor was still only eighteen years of age.

The work of preparing Victoria for the throne had been gathering pace. The Duchess had been granted £10,000 for the Princess's education, and she spent it well. No detail was overlooked. The queen-to-be was less than five feet tall, but that was no reason why she should not walk in a queenly manner. Somebody hit upon the idea of fixing a sprig of holly to the neck of her dress. It was hoped that this would make her walk with her head held high.

History was an important subject, but Victoria may

> "I felt that my confirmation was one of the most solemn and important events and acts in my life; and that I trusted that it might have a salutary effect on my mind." *Victoria after her confirmation*

have noticed that one page was always missing from her books. On it was printed a table showing the line of succession to the throne. With a craftiness which suggests Stockmar was behind it, the Duchess had decided that her daughter must not learn of her situation until the time was right.

The revelation occurred when Victoria was eleven. Her mother had come to the conclusion that her education should be tested on its fitness for a future Queen. The Bishops of London and Lincoln were asked to examine her in scripture, history, grammar, geography, arithmetic and Latin. She answered their questions with no great difficulty, and they pronounced her fit for any task which might lie ahead. To show their trust, they replaced the missing page in the history book. Strangely enough, Victoria had never seen herself as a future Queen, and the discovery made her unhappy. "I cried much on learning it," she confided to her diary. "I am nearer to the throne than I thought." To the bishops, she simply said: "I will be good."

There had been visits from German relatives – among them two young men from the House of Saxe-Coburg, the Princes Ernest and Albert. Victoria had preferred Albert. He was, she noted, "just as tall as Ernest but stouter [and] is extremely handsome." "His hair," she told the ever-eager pages of her journal, "is the colour of mine."

Apart from these diversions, she was growing up in a hothouse atmosphere, deprived of male company, and never out of the sight of Lehzen or her mother. She was a skilful artist, and she enjoyed visits to the opera – especially when an Italian piece was being performed. For the rest of it, this was a rather dull existence, in which there was everything but freedom.

On the night of the 19th June, 1837, she went to bed as usual in her mother's room. At five o'clock the following morning, there was a knocking on the door of the palace. The Archbishop of Canterbury, the Lord Chancellor, and the King's physician had arrived

Above Victoria, aged fifteen.

"Albert always used to have some fun and clever witty answer at breakfast and everywhere; he used to play and fondle Dash (her dog) so funnily too." *Victoria after a childhood encounter with her future husband*

15

> "I shall do my utmost to fulfil my duty towards my country; I am very young, and perhaps in many, though not in all things, inexperienced, but I am sure that very few have more real goodwill and more real desire to do what is fit and right than I have." *Victoria – on learning that she is Queen of England*

from Windsor Castle, where they had just witnessed the death of William IV. It was some time before they could summon a servant. Even when they were inside the building, the Duchess protested that her daughter was still asleep. At last, after an hour had gone by, a small figure came downstairs with a dressing-gown hastily flung over her nightdress.

The three men went down on their knees. Queen Victoria held out her hand to be kissed.

3 Learning to Rule

UNTIL UNCLE LEOPOLD accepted the crown of Belgium in 1830, he had spent much of his time at Claremont, the large house near Esher in Surrey where his wife had died. Victoria had enjoyed going to see him, and he had come as close as anyone could to replacing the father she had never known. Even after he had become King of Belgium, she wrote to him often. As soon as he heard about her accession to the throne, he was quick to offer advice. "The business of the highest in a state," he wrote to her, "is certainly, in my opinion, to act with great impartiality and a spirit of justice for the good of all."

As for Victoria herself, her new position gave a kind of freedom for which she had long yearned. In her diary that night, she wrote that "since it has pleased providence to place me into this station, I shall do my utmost to fulfil my duty towards my country." On hearing the news, however, her first reaction was of a much more practical kind. She asked her mother to "leave me by myself for an hour." Heaven knows what thoughts occurred to her during those sixty minutes. At the end of them, she issued her first order as Queen of England. It was – that her bed should be moved out of mama's room. Now, at long last, she was determined to enjoy a little privacy.

Victoria continued to look to Leopold as a father figure; but, within three hours of the visit by the Archbishop of Canterbury and the Lord Chamberlain, an even more imposing personage had come on to the scene. His name was Lord Melbourne. He was Victoria's first Prime Minister.

> "Poor little Queen, she is at an age at which a girl can hardly be trusted to choose a bonnet for herself; yet a task is laid upon her from which an archangel might shrink." *Thomas Carlyle*

Opposite Victoria, in her nightgown, learns from the Archbishop of Canterbury that she is Queen.

Lord Melbourne was a humourous, easy-going character, which was just as well. As Lady Caroline Lamb's husband, he had been compelled to endure her infatuation with Lord Byron, the romantic poet, and the madness that followed it. A more intense individual might have cracked under the strain, but Lord Melbourne carried on in his amiable way – almost as if nothing had happened.

As a politician, he was a member of the Liberal, or Whig, Party, but with Tory tendencies. "You'd better try to do no good, and then you'll get into no scrapes," he once advised a young Member of Parliament. At the time of Victoria's accession, he was not in a position to

Below Victoria riding with Lord Melbourne, her first Prime Minister.

do very much at all, for he ruled by a very slender majority.

However, if life had little to offer in Parliament, it provided more than enough compensation by giving him the task of schooling this young and highly-spirited monarch for her new responsibilities. The Queen loved him. She loved his courtesy, his wisdom, his humour, his calm, and his worldliness. He was everything a father should be, and perhaps more. His attitude to her was never anything but respectful; but, behind the reverence and clear enough for the Queen to see, there was real affection.

Outside the close confines of the court, the country adored its new sovereign. The idea of a girl Queen appealed enormously to its imagination: her freshness, her purity, made a welcome change after the insane babblings of George III's later years, and the boorish debaucheries of his sons. The rude Hanoverian clay, which had produced so many grotesques, had at last modelled a figure of unimagined beauty. In fact, Victoria was not beautiful and, with her short stature, not particularly impressive to look at; but the public was entranced. What reality could not produce in their Queen, her subjects fashioned in their imaginations.

Within one month of being proclaimed Queen, Victoria had moved into Buckingham Palace. Her spaniel, Darby, liked the garden there, which was a happy omen. Less happy, perhaps, was the fact that she insisted on settling her mother at the far end of the building. The apparent insult became more obvious when the Duchess learned that Louise Lehzen had been put into quarters next door to the Queen's, and that a connecting doorway was to be made. If, during her sleep, the sovereign had nightmares, it would be to the German governess that she would turn.

Her removal to the far side of the palace rankled with the Duchess. The pink-cheeked bride of the Duke of Kent had become a bitter middle-aged woman who bickered endlessly on matters of court protocol. As a

"I have no doubt he is passionately fond of her as he might be of his daughter if he had one; and the more because he is a man with a capacity for loving without having anything in the world to love." *Charles Greville on Melbourne's attitude to Queen Victoria*

nineteenth birthday present for Victoria, she purchased a copy of *King Lear*, with its vicious portrayal of two un-dutiful daughters. In spite of Melbourne's assurances that it was "a very fine play," the meaning of the gift must have been obvious.

But, apart from the squabbles with mama, the first months of Victoria's reign were an idyllic period. "It was," she wrote, "the pleasantest summer I EVER passed in *my life*." Nor was that of the following year any less wonderful. On 28th June, 1838, her coronation was due to take place. It was, perhaps, proof of the nation's feelings that Parliament agreed to spend £200,000 on it. William IV had only been granted £50,000 for his celebrations.

Compared with the well rehearsed modern version of a coronation, there was something very amateurish about the occasion. The only advice given to the Archbishop of Canterbury was to "put the crown on firmly." The Queen slept badly the night before; but Lord Melbourne, who was at Buckingham Palace early, was quick to reassure her that she would enjoy herself – once she reached Westminster Abbey. The day began with rain; but, as the young Queen climbed into the state coach, the sun came out. It was, everyone agreed, a good omen.

Of all the peers present at the Abbey, only two knew how to put on their robes correctly. There was some unseemly mirth during the cremony when a nona-genarian baron named John Rolle fell over as he went to pay homage. The Archbishop put the ring on the wrong finger; the Bishop of Bath and Wells turned over two pages in the prayer book by mistake; and, when the Queen went into St. Edward's Chapel, she found the altar littered with sandwiches and bottles of wine.

Nevertheless, there were some wonderful moments – as when she caught Lehzen's eye in the Abbey, and they exchanged smiles which were full of understanding; and she felt proud to look at the pillars decorated in crimson and gold, and the great throng of people who had come to pay tribute to her inside and outside the

Above Victoria in her coronation regalia, and *opposite*, she is anointed with oil by the Archbishop of Canterbury.

Abbey. As one observer said, she was "gay as a lark, like a girl on her birthday."

When it was all over, and she returned to the palace, her first action was to hurry upstairs to her private apartments. It was time to give her dog its bath.

Those were indeed happy days, with Lord Melbourne always there to guide her, and a growing assurance of her ability to rule. She used to spend the mornings going over the documents that needed her approval, sent by the various government departments. In the afternoons, there would be long rides, with Melbourne beside her, and anything up to thirty in the party. Afterwards, she used to play with the children of her courtiers in the palace corridors before the time came to dress for dinner.

In the days of the uncle kings, the evening meal had been followed by a riot of hard drinking and gambling. With the new monarch, no such excesses were allowed. Conversation in the drawing room was formal, even stiff. Victoria made a point of talking to every guest, and some of the meetings were very heavy going.

Later, however, everyone relaxed. Above all, the Queen loved to dance. When there were no opportunities, she played games of spillikins (pick-up-sticks) and, frequently, chess. Her opponents were, perhaps, unfortunate, for she had Melbourne and the other cabinet ministers to help her. Even so, she did not always win. Once she recorded, "Aunt Louise triumphed over my Council of Ministers." The games lasted until half-past eleven, when everybody retired to bed.

Her only fear was Melbourne's tiny majority in the House of Commons, and the dread that, one day, he might be replaced. "I shall be very sorry to lose him *even* for *one* night," she wrote. And: "HOW *sad* I feel, when I think of the POSSIBILITY of this excellent and truly kind man not *remaining* my minister!" She probably confided these doubts and fears to Lehzen. To the rest of the world, she seemed to be full of confidence, no matter what fate might produce in the

way of Prime Ministers. As was soon painfully clear, she had little cause for such faith. Victoria's problems were about to begin.

Above Victoria's first Privy Council meeting. Lord Melbourne is standing, with pen and papers.

4 The First Clouds

KING LEOPOLD HAD RECOMMENDED Christian Stockmar to the Duchess of Kent as a man of wisdom. The fact that he happened to be a doctor as well was incidental. For medical purposes, Leopold suggested that his sister should consult a middle-aged practitioner named Sir James Clark.

Clark was a Scotsman who had trained at Aberdeen University. For a number of years, he had been a naval surgeon. He had attended John Keats during the poet's final illness and, more recently, he had been appointed to Leopold's household. His skill at diagnosis was, to say the least, limited. He believed in plenty of fresh air, and prescribed "simple remedies." He was not a very good doctor.

All the same, Leopold believed in him; so did the Duchess, and so (more's the pity) did Victoria. He presently became dragged into the feud between the Queen and her mother. The result was disastrous.

Among the Duchess of Kent's friends was an attractive spinster named Lady Flora Hastings. Victoria and Lehzen mistrusted her, for she was an intimate of Sir John Conroy, who was trying to worm his way into a position of power. She was travelling down from Scotland with Sir John, when she became ill. She visited Clark, who gave her some pills.

A few days later, Victoria and Lehzen were talking about Lady Flora's ailment. Her figure, they had observed, seemed to be changing. She appeared, not to put too fine a point on it, to be "filling out." Together, the two women uttered the dire word *pregnant*. Had this confidante of the Duchess of Kent been spending her

Above Sir James Clark, Victoria's court doctor.

Above Chartist demonstrators march to Parliament with their Great National Petition, which demanded a vote for every man and other reforms.

spare time in a manner unsuitable for a lady-in-wating? A rumour was born which, in the tittle-tattling circles of court, spread rapidly. Lady Flora was asked about her condition. She agreed that Clark should examine her, in the interests of truth and her reputation.

Had Clark been a more able medical man, the matter would have ended there. Possibly there would have been apologies and, before long, everybody would have forgotten about it. But Clark, either because he was a fool, or because he believed in satisfying the conscience of the Crown, didn't give a straight answer. Lady Flora was, he stated, a virgin. On the other hand, he managed to imply, a pregnancy was not impossible. The court seemed to overlook the fact that the only precedent for such a statement was at the beginning of the New Testament, and the tongues wagged even more rapidly.

Lady Flora Hastings was not pregnant. As time went on, she became more and more ill, until it was found

Above Sir Robert Peel speaking in the House of Commons.

that she had a tumour on the liver. The poor woman died: Sir James Clark was deserted by nearly all his patients except those in the Royal Household, and the first blemish occurred on Victoria's popular reputation.

There was more trouble to follow. Melbourne's position as Prime Minister was becoming more and more difficult, until his command of Parliament was reduced to a majority of five. He was unwilling to struggle painfully on when eventual defeat was certain, so he handed in his resignation. In 1839, Sir Robert Peel was asked to form a Cabinet.

Peel was a Tory, and Victoria mistrusted Tories. He was shy, and difficult to understand at first; even though he treated Victoria with great respect, she felt ill at ease with him.

Discomfort gave way to anger, when Peel raised the question of the Ladies of the Bedchamber. These ladies-in-waiting had all been appointed on the advice of Melbourne and so, not unnaturally, they were staunch Whigs. Their husbands were Whigs, their brothers were Whigs, and, as Peel pointed out, it would be a poor thing for the Head of Government if the Head of State were surrounded by persuasive relatives of the Opposition. The Queen must get rid of them, and appoint ladies whose sympathies were more in tune with the ideas of the Government.

Victoria refused. Melbourne, to his credit, advised her to do as Peel asked, but the Queen had put her foot down. "Sir Robert Peel," she wrote to Melbourne, "has behaved very ill; he insisted on my giving up my ladies, to which I replied that I *never* would consent, and I never saw a man so frightened." Even the Duke of Wellington, the victor of Waterloo and the last Tory Prime Minister, whose opinion was not to be ignored, failed to convince her. The Queen was acting unconstitutionally, but her rage put her past caring.

Sadly, Sir Robert informed her that, under the circumstances, he was unable to form a Government. Melbourne was hauled back for a further term as Prime Minister. A ball was held, and Her Majesty looked happy once more. Peel and the Duke of Wellington, who were present, looked rather less than delighted.

The reign which had begun with all the light and the promise of a spring morning was now becoming clouded. Within the palace, relations between the Queen and the Duchess of Kent had grown so bad that, when Victoria sent her mother a note meant to make up the quarrel, the Duchess refused to believe that she had written it. Outside in the streets, the young monarch's popularity had slumped dramatically. When the public heard about the death of Lady Flora Hastings, they shouted the words "Mrs. Melbourne!" at her. The aspersion was quite unjustified, but it hurt. She was hissed when she went to the races at Ascot. Indeed, the only thing upon which everybody was agreed was that she should get married as soon as possible. For most people, it was the time-honoured remedy for all women who seemed to be behaving foolishly. For some, however, the demand stemmed from fear of the Queen's death. If she were to die without an heir, the throne would pass to her supposedly wicked uncle, the Duke of Cumberland. Nobody wanted a return to the dark days of Hanoverian debauchery.

How, then, should a suitable marriage be arranged? Uncle Leopold, even though he was now King of the Belgians, still liked to have a finger in every pie, and it was to him that they turned. Leopold had no doubt. There was only one man who had "every quality that could be desired to render her perfectly happy." The young man's name was Prince Albert of Saxe-Coburg.

"I was calm but very decided, and I think you would have been pleased to see my composure and great firmness; the Queen of England will not submit to such trickery." *Victoria, recalling her attitude when Sir Robert Peel asked her to dismiss her pro-Whig Ladies of the Bedchamber*

"Nobody cares for the Queen, her popularity has sunk to zero, and loyalty is a dead letter." *Charles Greville quoted in the* Morning Post, *25th March, 1839*

5 A Royal Romance

THE QUEEN, HERSELF, WAS IN NO HURRY to get married. In April, 1839, she told Melbourne that "at present *my* feeling is against ever marrying." Had she decided to model herself on Elizabeth I? If so, she was making a mistake. She had little of her ancestor's tyranny, and the relations between monarch and people had changed considerably since those days. In any case, Victoria was a woman who felt the need to have a man around. Possibly it was because she had never known a father; at all events, from Leopold to Melbourne to Albert and beyond, there was always a man in her life to whom she looked for support.

At the time when she addressed her remark to the Prime Minister, Prince Albert of Saxe-Coburg had been touring Italy with Christian Stockmar as his companion. When it was suggested that she might, at least, see the young man, Victoria protested that there could be no talk of an engagement; and that, even if she liked him, nothing could possibly happen for the next two or three years.

In the end, however, she gave way a little. A meeting could take place, and, on the 10th October, 1839, Albert and his brother Ernest presented themselves at Windsor Castle.

The Queen may have been unsure whether she would even like Albert, but his feelings about her were equally lukewarm. As children, they had met several times, and the memories failed to kindle even the smallest spark of passion – or even affection. Victoria, he felt, was a young woman who enjoyed ceremony and late nights and flirtatious gossip, and didn't care for nature

> "I said, Why need I marry at all for 3 or 4 years? Did he see the necessity? . . . I said I dreaded the thought of marrying; that I was so accustomed to have my own way, that I thought it 10 to 1 that I shouldn't agree with anybody." *Victoria, recalling a conversation with Lord Melbourne*

> "The young man ought to have not merely great ability, but a *right* ambition, and great force of will as well. To pursue for a lifetime a political career so arduous demands more than energy and inclination – it demands also that earnest frame of mind which is ready of its own accord to sacrifice mere pleasure to real usefulness." *Christian Stockmar on the qualities needed in the Queen's husband*

Opposite Albert, the Prince Consort, in his uniform as a Field Marshal.

and wild life and the things which interested him. She would, he believed, be a most unsuitable wife for such a serious person as he was.

Albert was, indeed, very serious. He was, as it happened, Victoria's first cousin. He had been educated at Bonn University and in Brussels, but most of all he enjoyed wandering through the woods near his home at Rosenau, collecting samples of natural history. He loved music passionately, but he found politics dull. His parents had been divorced, and his mother had died unhappily in Paris back in 1831. He was three months younger than Victoria.

King Leopold, who felt very sure of his judgement, had told Albert that, some day, "the little English May-flower" would be his bride. Since then he had never seriously, thought about marrying anyone else. But, to be honest, he had not thought much about marrying the English Mayflower, either.

This, then, was the young man who arrived at

Below A drawing by Prince Albert of Reinhardtsbrunn House, Gotha.

Windsor Castle with his brother on that autumn day in 1839. He was tall, with blue eyes and (to quote the Queen) "an exquisite nose, and such a pretty mouth with delicate moustachios and slight but very slight whiskers." His brother Ernest, she noted, "is grown quite handsome; Albert's *beauty* is *most striking*, and he is so amiable and unaffected – in short, very *fascinating*." In short, she fell hopelessly in love with him.

He arrived on a Thursday. By the following Monday, she made up her mind to marry him.

Albert, in spite of all his doubts, had come to the same conclusion. Whatever worries Victoria may have had about the rightness of a woman, even the Queen of England, proposing to a man, were quickly dispelled. She said her piece, briefly and beautifully. Albert replied with a torrent of German phrases, all of which added up to "I love you." Then he wrapped his arms around her. The Prince from Saxe-Coburg had found his Mayflower at last. What was no less important for the future, was the fact he had also felt the first intoxicating symptoms of ambition.

It was agreed that they should be married in the following February, 1840. Meanwhile, Albert and Ernest would go home to Germany, where the bridegroom-to-be would meditate about his future role, and take his farewell of his beloved woods and hills around Rosenau.

There was much to be settled. The Queen, in her first rapture, decided that Albert should be given the title of King Consort. Nobody would have dared to laugh at her, but the idea was out of the question. The British constitution made no provision for such a title, and it was certainly not going to be rewritten just because the sovereign was infatuated with this German princeling. At last it was decided that he should not even be made a member of the peerage. The Army was prepared to make him a Field Marshal, but the Royal Navy refused to appoint him an Admiral of the Fleet. The Navy slipped several degrees in the Queen's estimation – as did anybody who thought dearest Albert less

"I said to him, that I thought he must be aware *why* I wished them to come here, – and that it would make me *too happy* if he would consent to what I wished (to marry me)." *Victoria on her proposal to Prince Albert*

Below Photography was still in its infancy when Victoria and Albert were married, but in 1854 they posed in their wedding clothes for this picture.

than perfect.

So far as money was concerned, Victoria reminded her ministers that, when Leopold married George IV's daughter, he had been given an annual allowance of £50,000 (worth about £400,000 at present-day prices). The same sum, she felt, would be right for Albert. The Tories in Parliament thought otherwise. Many of the people of England were desperately poor; and, even if they granted him £30,000 a year, it would be a good deal more than the total revenue of Coburg. This confirmed the Queen's dislike of the perfidious Tories, but she was bound to agree. Thirty thousand pounds a year it had to be.

As for matters of court precedence, the Duke of Cumberland refused to bow to a man whom he described as "a paper Royal Highness." True to the Queen's idea of them as villains, the Tory politicians agreed with him. "Poor dear Albert," Victoria lamented to her journal, "how cruelly are they ill-using that dearest Angel! Monsters! You Tories shall be punished. Revenge, revenge!"

There was no revenge. Far from punishing the Tories, the last slender shreds of Melbourne's power had disintegrated. Five months after the marriage of Victoria and Albert in February, Sir Robert Peel was asked to form a cabinet. Among its members were seven past or future prime ministers and five future viceroys of India. The affair of the Ladies of the Bedchamber was forgotten. Melbourne, who was growing old, ambled off into retirement, but it no longer mattered. Victoria had Albert, and that was enough.

The Queen's attitude to politics was nothing if not flexible. She came to realize that Peel was not as unpleasant as she had first thought, and the Whigs gradually slid out of favour. Conservatism was now the thing, though the crisis of Corn Law repeal in 1846 must have made the whole political set-up seem very curious to her straightforward mind. Peel was opposed by his own party over measures to provide cheaper food which, considering the state of Britain's larder,

Above The wedding of Victoria and Albert in the Chapel Royal, Windsor Castle.

especially the starvation caused by potato blight in Ireland, were vital. Had it not been for the support of the opposition, the Act would never have got through Parliament. What was she to make of that? What no doubt troubled her most was that this most unhappy Prime Minister, on whom she now lavished her trust, was compelled to resign soon afterwards, and later joined the Liberal Party.

6 The New Régime

Below Christian Stockmar, Albert's doctor and adviser.

BARONESS LEHZEN, who had come to the Duchess of Kent's as a simple governess, had gained power as her charge grew up. She had been given a title and had been put in charge of the Queen's private income, the Privy Purse. And wherever Albert went, Stockmar usually went too. Previously the doctor and counsellor's appearances at court had been largely confined to the deaths of kings and princesses. Now, he moved in more or less permanently. Three ladies-in-waiting conveniently announced their resignations when the Whigs went out of office, but the Queen no longer minded. Albert was there, and that was what mattered. As she told her journal, "My dearest angel is indeed a great comfort to me."

Albert, himself, needed comfort at this time. He was shy, awkward, and, according to common opinion, did not look English. He walked with a slight droop, and he seemed pathetically anxious not to make mistakes. The English people seemed suspicious of him as they were of *all* foreigners. Also, only Victoria appreciated his jokes, which was not really surprising. Whatever sense of fun he may have had was not supported by a sense of humour. They were, on the whole, very bad jokes.

Nor was the Royal honeymoon spirit allowed to endure for long. The Queen could be irritable, and Albert had more than his fair share of Teutonic stubbornness. On one occasion, so the story goes, the young couple quarrelled. Albert went off in a temper, and locked himself in his room. Victoria was the quicker to relent. Before long, there was a knock on his door. "Who's there?" he asked. "The Queen of

England," Victoria replied. Nothing happened. She knocked again, and again Albert asked who was there. This time, she answered "Your wife, Albert." He opened the door.

In their relationship, and in the upbringing of the royal children, she always made one thing perfectly clear. She might be Head of State, but he was the head of the family. In spite of her own often imperious attitude, she firmly believed that a woman should have a man as her master. "We women were not *made* for governing," she once said. Curiously enough she probably meant it!

During one crisis, she indignantly said: "I should like to know if they mean to give the *Ladies* seats in Parliament." She was firmly opposed to any suggestion that women should be allowed to vote. Indeed, many years later, when she read a newspaper report about a talk on women's suffrage delivered to the Mechanic's Institute at Slough, she was extremely angry. The speaker, she noted, "ought to get a *good whipping.*"

She was also opposed to the advancement of her sex in the professions. After a great many struggles, a lady named Elizabeth Garrett achieved the distinction of becoming Britain's first woman doctor. One day, Victoria's daughter, Louise, visited Dr. Garrett at her home. After an interesting talk, the Princess came away – having begged her host not to tell mama about her visit. In fact, Queen Victoria did hear about the meeting, and was most annoyed. On another occasion, she threatened to withdraw her patronage from a medical congress, if women were allowed to attend.

Victoria's opinions are proably best summed up in her own words, thus: "The Queen is most anxious to enlist everyone who can speak or write, to join in checking this mad, wicked, folly of 'Women's Rights' with all its attendant horrors...It is a subject which makes the Queen so furious that she cannot contain herself...Woman would become the most hateful, heartless, and disgusting of human beings were she allowed to unsex herself, and where would be the

"The Prince has improved very much lately. He has evidently a head for politics. He has become, too, far more independent. His mental activity is constantly on the increase, and he gives the greater part of his time to business, without complaining." *Stockmar on Prince Albert*

"What an *awful* idea this is – of allowing *young girls* and young men to enter the dissecting room together." *Victoria, opposing the idea of permitting women to become doctors*

Below Victoria as she appeared on the world's first postage stamp, the Penny Black of 1840.

Above The Queen and Prince Consort posed frequently for the early photographers.

protection which man was intended to give the weaker sex?"

Albert was certainly not lacking in protective qualities, and the Queen rejoiced in them. She adapted herself to him: to his stiff principles and his stern views on morality (possibly brought about by the unhappy story of his parents). The fun-loving Queen, who used to dance all night, had vanished. The age of Victorian prudery had begun.

But Albert brought more than new standards of straight-laced behaviour: he brought ideas. He studied books about politics and English law, and found them much more interesting than he had expected. He got on famously with Sir Robert Peel, which at once changed his wife's views on the Tory Prime Minister. If Albert approved of Peel, and he approved of Albert, there was no more to be said. Above all, Albert brought his love of art and music and science with him. The cultural scene in England was about to be transformed, and there were few undertakings which did not bear the mark of his design – from the house which the royal couple built at Osborne on the Isle of Wight, to the arrangements for the Duke of Wellington's funeral in 1852.

In the latter project, the Prince's ideas may have seemed rather extravagant. The Duke, for all his high military reputation, was a mere five feet tall. Nevertheless, the coffin (designed by the Prince) which rode on top of the huge bronze funeral carriage (also designed by the prince) was six feet nine inches long.

The Queen thought it was most appropriate; but, then, she agreed with her husband on most things. She even submitted on what might have been a very tricky problem – the future of Baroness Lehzen. Prince Albert hated the former governess, whom he described as "a crazy, common, stupid intriguer." Eventually – as Lehzen's power seemed to lessen under the Prince's influence, and as the Royal children were born – she was sent to live with a sister in Germany. She took with her a pension of £300 a year and countless photographs of the Queen.

> "*Great* events make me quiet and calm; it is only trifles that irritate my nerves." *Queen Victoria*

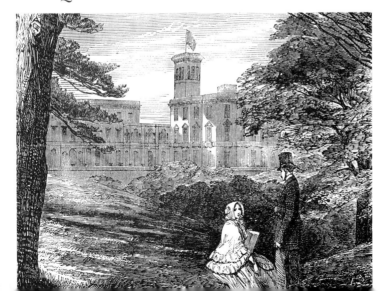

Left Osborne, on the Isle of Wight, where the royal couple spent most of every summer.

7 The Great Exhibition

THE NEW EPOCH, which followed Prince Albert's view of life, embraced as its cardinal virtues duty, industry, morality and domesticity. Nobody supported them more fervently than the Queen herself. Somehow, she believed, there had to be a symbol of these new attitudes, and of Britain's progress since her uncles' reigns: a grand demonstration of what could be regarded as Prince Albert's manifesto. Eventually, and the idea **was** essentially Albert's, it was decided that there should be a great exhibition – or, rather, *the* Great Exhibition. The year was 1851.

Below A typical early Victorian industrial scene – the opening of new docks at Briton Ferry, Glamorgan.

A site was chosen by the Prince himself in Hyde Park. The display was to be more magnificent than anything ever seen before, and it was to be international. Every country was to be invited to show examples of its products, raw materials, machinery, and arts. Out of the profits, a permanent museum was to be built.

Albert's beliefs inspired the Great Exhibition, and his imagination and enthusiasm brought it about. Nevertheless, it might be argued, there was something inevitable about this huge display of the world's industry. It was, perhaps, a statement about the condition of Britain midway through the 19th Century. On the one hand, it was an admission that the United Kingdom was no longer a tight little island, whose farmers and manufacturers could protect themselves with tariff barriers and the Royal Navy against the rest of the globe. On the other, there was a note of defiance about it. Whatever the others can do, it seemed to say, we can do better.

The statement was, to some extent, true. The repeal of the Corn Laws in 1846 had been brought about by the high prices of food in the towns, and by the disastrous potato famines in Ireland. If the Queen's subjects, of whom there were a million more every four years, were to be well nourished, the nation's farmers could no longer be protected against foreign competition. Corn from abroad must be allowed to pour in. Britain could no longer grow enough food to satisfy its hungry people. It had to buy all it could get: from the Empire, if possible; if not, then from all corners of the world.

For a poor country, this might have been a disaster. Britain, however, could afford to pay for what it wanted. With the coming of steam, British engineers had released the pent-up wealth of their genius. The country was served by an ever-growing network of railways. When a foreign country decided to build a rail system, it was usually to British resources and British brains, that the government in question turned. On the high seas, her steamships were setting standards for speed, comfort and reliability. What with this and the booming

> "The first of May (opening day of the Great Exhibition) was the *greatest* day in our history, the most *beautiful* and imposing and *touching* spectacle ever seen, and the triumph of my beloved Albert." *Victoria*

"The Chinese commissioner, insensibly touched with the solemnity of the scene during the Hallelujah Chorus, was taking his way slowly round the margin of the fountain and making a prostration before Her Majesty." *An account of the opening ceremony of the Great Exhibition*

factories of the North and Midlands, there was, indeed, much to celebrate. The Great Exhibition was the ultimate in this respect.

Two hundred and thirty-four plans were submitted for the buildings. One was by a man named Joseph Paxton. Albert knew about Paxton, who had worked as a gardener for the Duke of Devonshire. Some years earlier, when he and Victoria had visited the Duke's estate at Chatsworth in Derbyshire, he had admired the large conservatories. These were Paxton's creations. Suddenly, Albert knew what to do. The Great Exhibition, should be housed in a crystal palace – a giant building made from glass – and Paxton should be the designer.

Sir Robert Peel was enthusiastic about the idea, which was more than could be said of everyone. Led by *The Times*, there was an outcry against the use of Hyde Park for what was obviously *trade*. The fashionable residents of Belgravia and Mayfair, who exercised their horses and their children in the Park, were unwilling to see the source of their wealth at such close quarters. It was the success of the Exhibition that did much to change this attitude.

There was a shortage of money; and not until £200,000 had been subscribed to a guarantee fund was it possible to go ahead. Even then, there were difficulties. The birds of Britain found their way into the great glass exhibition hall; and, as birds will, added their own unwelcome decorations to the exhibits of all nations. The Duke of Wellington produced the best solution to this problem. Asked for advice by the Queen, he snapped: "Sparrow-hawks, Ma'am."

On 1st May, 1851, everything was ready. The Archbishop of Canterbury uttered a short prayer. The Queen, terribly excited, cut the tape, and a choir of six hundred burst into the Hallelujah Chorus from Handel's *Messiah*.

A number of people argued that the glass roof would be unsafe; and, although six million people visited the exhibition there were, significantly, no crowned heads

from other countries present.

It did not escape popular notice that this orgy of glass construction had happened in the same year as Window Tax was repealed. Nor did the President of the Bible Society overlook the text on the Exhibition catalogue. On Albert's insistence it bore the words: "The Earth is the Lord's and all that therein is." As the President rightly pointed out, this was the prayer book version and not the Bible's. It may have seemed to be a stupid quibble, but quibbling was a favourite nineteenth century pastime.

However, there were a great many things to be admired – among them two model dwellings for members of the working classes, which had been built in the grounds. If the machines and the nuts and bolts

Above Victoria and Albert at the opening of the Great Exhibition. Behind them is the Duke of Wellington.

"I could not believe it was the last time I was to see it. An organ, accompanied by a fine and powerful wind instrument called the sommerophone, was being played, and it nearly upset me. The canvas is very dirty, the red curtains are faded and many things are very much soiled, still the effect is fresh and new as ever and most beautiful." *Victoria on her last visit to the Great Exhibition*

symbolized industry, these stood for domesticity and morals. They expressed most suitably Albert's statement to the world, and gave a more homely touch to the vision of Utopia he had caused to be built in Hyde Park.

At last the show was over, the final day falling on the twelfth anniversary of His Royal Highness's betrothal to Victoria. That night, the Queen wrote in her diary: "Albert's dearest name is immortalized with this *great* conception, *his* own, and my *own* dear country showed she was *worthy* of it."

No doubt about it: the Exhibition was the high point in Albert's career as Consort. It showed that, in spirit at any rate, he belonged to that select company of artist-engineers – men such as Isambard Kingdom Brunel who built the Great Western Railway and the *Great Eastern* steamship – who were such inspired leaders of nineteenth century progress.

The Great Exhibition ended, but its spirit did not. Out of the substantial profits, a site was purchased between Kensington Gardens and Cromwell Road in London. Following an idea of Prince Albert's, it was to be put to educational use. In 1856, work on the first of the buildings began. It was designed by Sir William Cubitt as an art gallery. When complete, its construction of glass and iron vaults inspired the nickname of "Brompton Boilers." The collection of Victorian art has moved to the Tate Gallery; but part of "Brompton Boilers" still exists. It has been rebuilt as a museum at Bethnal Green. On the Kensington site, in a flamboyant Eastern style that would not have pleased the Prince's severe taste, now stands the Victoria and Albert Museum.

Is it a law of existence that every moment of happiness, every success, must be followed by something dismal? Victoria and her husband had been made immeasurably contented by the success of the Great Exhibition, but troubles lay ahead – in the shape of Lord Palmerston and the Crimean War.

8 War Clouds

PRINCE ALBERT HAD GIVEN THE WORLD proof of his ability, but he was still not popular in so-called "high circles." The trouble was that he was too *intense*: he had to have a purpose in everything he did. Even when he showed his ability to ride to hounds with the best of them, he spoilt it all by suggesting that it was a waste of time, and that it bored him. He did not, he explained, ride for amusement. The Prince did very few things for amusement.

All this gave society's upper crust ample opportunity to say that he was no sportsman – that, in a word, he was un-English. One doubts whether Albert minded this criticism very much. He did not, indeed, *want* to be like the English. He much preferred the company of Christian Stockmar and his old friends back in Coburg.

When Lord Palmerston made his courtly be-whiskered way into the orbit of Albert's political awareness, the Prince did not approve of him. Some years earlier, the statesman had been found in bed with a lady-in-waiting at Windsor Castle. The incident was frowned upon, but it in no way hindered his political career. Palmerston had been a Tory Cabinet Minister at the age of twenty-two, and when, in 1830, he was appointed Foreign Secretary, he held office for the greater part of eleven years. It was a record.

In the days of William IV, Palmerston had submitted all his dispatches to the monarch, who often rewrote them. When Victoria came to the throne, he felt that his moment of freedom had arrived. He would not show his intentions to the new sovereign, who would in any case probably not understand them. It would re-

"The loyalty and enthusiasm of the inhabitants are great; but the heat is greater still. I am satisfied that if the population of Liverpool had been weighed this morning, and were to be weighed again now, they would be many degrees lighter."
Prince Albert after opening the Albert Dock, Liverpool, during a heatwave

43

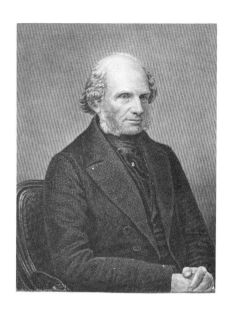

Above, the peace-loving Lord John Russell, and *below*, the bellicose Lord Palmerston, the two Liberal statesmen who dominated British politics for twenty years.

lieve him of a tedious duty, and enable him to indulge in his favourite diplomatic pastime of driving the country dangerously – without actually allowing it to collide with another power.

With the Prince to guide her, Victoria's views on Palmerston changed. In the early years, she had enjoyed his company. She found him charming: he advised her during her games of chess, and he often joined the afternoon riding parties. But that was another Victoria, and one who might have overlooked his moment of weakness at Windsor Castle.

The Victoria of Albert's influence was sterner. The fall from grace was to be neither forgiven nor forgotten. She began to resent Palmerston's failure to seek her approval, and Albert was asked to draft a memorandum informing the minister of her new attitude. Palmerston apologized, and did nothing about it. He was rebuked: more apologies and, again, no action. In 1848, she asked the Prime Minister, Lord John Russell, to dismiss him. Russell hesitated. Palmerston was very popular in the House of Commons, and Russell was afraid to get rid of him. He took no action, and hoped that the Queen and her husband would get over it. Two hundred years after the beheading of Charles I, it was still not clear how far the monarch could interfere in the running of the country.

In 1848, one might have been surprised at the sovereign taking such a strong line, for it had been a bad year for monarchy. In France, Louis-Philippe had been forced to abdicate; there had been a rising in Vienna; Karl Marx and Friedrich Engels were writing their *Communist Manifesto* in London; and a colossal demonstration of working class solidarity assembled in Kennington, London, by the Chartists was halted at Westminster Bridge by bad weather and two hundred special constables (among whom was the future Napoleon III of France).

Before his death in 1852, one of the Duke of Wellington's last actions had been to offer Prince Albert the post of Commander-in-Chief of the Army. The

Prince had turned it down on the grounds that it would leave him too little time to spend with his wife. It was something which, two years later, both he and the nation (though the nation did not realize it) should have regretted. If the capable, efficient Albert had been in charge, he would never have let the service degenerate into the run-down, cumbersome and antiquated machine which got itself involved in the Crimean War.

Since Lord Palmerston was serving as Home Secretary at the time, he might have disclaimed responsibility for the collision with Russia over Turkey. However it was he who forced the Prime Minister, Lord Aberdeen, to anger the Russians by his inflammatory speeches in the Commons – and he who had whipped up popular enthusiasm by writing letters to the *Morning Post*. The vehicle of state was at last

"I said that I thought that Lord Palmerston often endangered the honour of England by taking a very prejudiced and one-sided view of a question; that his writings were always as bitter as gall and did great harm."
Queen Victoria in a memorandum to Lord John Russell

Above Stores and ammunition piled up on the docks at Balaclava, in the Crimea, despite desperate shortages in the front line.

"They were so touched, so pleased; many, I hear, cried – and they won't hear of giving up their medals to have their names engraved upon them for fear they should *not* receive the *identical one* **put into** *their hands by me,* **which is quite touching."**
Queen Victoria, after presenting medals to soldiers who fought in the Crimean War

involved in an accident, but Lord Palmerston did not have it on his conscience. After all, he had not been driving.

Many Britons hated the Turkish sultan, Abdul-Mejîd, for the way he treated the Slavs and Bulgarians under Turkish rule. Palmerston, however, was right to be suspicious when the Tsar said of Turkey, "We have on our hands a very sick man – it will be a great misfortune if one of these days he should slip away from us." Certainly the Russians would have liked to capture Constantinople, which would have made life difficult for the Royal Navy in the Mediterranean. The cause of the war, though, was a silly quarrel over protection of the Holy Places in Jerusalem; and before the British and French troops had actually reached the East, the Russians had withdrawn from Turkish territory.

As Britain and France were drawn into this quarrel which need not have concerned them, life for Victoria and Albert became much harder. Palmerston, the **rogue** minister, was the man of the moment. The Royal couple, and Albert in particular, were known to oppose him – and what was Albert? A foreigner. The public brow contorted in a frown. Rumours began to multiply. One account had it that the Queen and her husband had both been arrested. Another said that Albert had been imprisoned in the Tower of London. A good many people believed it, and an angry crowd assembled at the gates.

Once war had actually broken out, however, all this was forgotten. The Queen, who looked on the Army as a personal possession, became anxious for the welfare of the troops. She applauded the efforts of Florence Nightingale to lessen the sufferings of the sick and wounded; instituted the Victoria Cross as an award for valour; visited countless hospitals; and presented medals from a dais in the Horse Guards Parade. According to one officer, a visit from Her Majesty was better than promotion. The Queen's main impression was of how young her soldiers were. "I own I feel as if these were *my own children*," she wrote to her uncle King Leopold;

"my heart beats for them as for my *nearest and dearest*!"

As for Prince Albert, he was applying his administrative talents to suggesting improvements to the fighting services and the conduct of the war. On his advice, a troop depot was set up on Malta; regular reports were sent back on the condition of the men outside the besieged Russian naval base at Sebastopol: and a camp was set up in the United Kingdom where several regiments could stay and train together. It was the germ which created Aldershot.

In 1855, Aberdeen's government was destroyed by its own incompetence, and Palmerston was made Prime Minister. Queen Victoria was nothing if not flexible in her emotions. She now found that she quite liked him; and, when at last the war was over, she rewarded him the Order of the Garter. Her rapid powers of forgiveness were even extended to Nicholas I, the Tsar of Russia, who died in 1855. Once Sebastopol had been captured, the British and French withdrew without keeping any of the territory they had occupied, and made peace. The Queen forgot that she had held Nicholas, and no one else, responsible for the Crimean War. She remembered only his personal kindness.

Left Victoria, Albert, and their two eldest sons listen to a wounded soldier telling of his experiences in the Crimea.

9 The Royal Family

NINETEENTH CENTURY BRITAIN was a land of violent contrasts: of an affluent middle class whose prosperity depended on the ill-paid labours of those whom Victoria was apt to describe (affectionately) as "the lowest of the low." Prince Albert had been warned by his advisers to live without too much expensive display. Otherwise, they said the, left-wing press could compare palace luxury with working-class poverty.

His Royal Highness did his best to comply. He and the Queen also tried to overcome cases of hardship. In 1842, for instance, a costume ball was held at Buckingham Palace in aid of the unemployed silk weavers of Spitalfields, London. Again, after a serious outbreak of fever in the industrial regions, the Prince set up a "Commission for Investigating the Sanitary Conditions of the Labouring Classes." Two "respectable men" of Belper, who asked the Prince to wear short trousers to help the stocking industry, received less satisfaction. In an age when some people considered that even to expose the legs of a chair was indecent, a public display of the royal limbs would have horrified the Queen.

In their domestic life, the Royal couple were a very model of respectability. The country's aristocracy might search endlessly for pleasure, but the highest household in the land cultivated hard work and sober living. It was an example that their middle class subjects made a brave pretence of following.

All told, Victoria and Albert had nine children, not an unusual number at the time. The first to arrive was Victoria, Princess Royal (fondly known as "Vicky"), who was born in 1840. The Prince of Wales (later

"You may well join us in thanking God for joining to us all our dearest, perfect Father . . . *None* of you can *ever* be proud enough of being the *child* of SUCH a Father who has not his *equal* in this world – so great, so good, so faultless." *Victoria in a letter to the Prince of Wales*

Opposite (l. to r.) Alfred, Prince Albert, Hélène, Louise, Arthur, Beatrice, Queen Victoria, the Princess Royal, Louise, Leopold and the Prince of Wales

Opposite All royal occasions were marked by national celebrations – here Edinburgh is lit up in honour of Prince Alfred's wedding.

Below The Queen's children were made to work – the Prince of Wales inspects a colliery at Shireoaks, Nottinghamshire.

"She spoke a good deal about the Princes and bade me notice two peculiarities in the Prince of Wales. First, at times he hangs his head and looks at his feet ... Secondly, riding hard, or after he has become fatigued, has been invariably followed by outbursts of temper." *The Prince of Wales's tutor, on the Queen's instructions to him*

Edward VII) was born in the following year. The last of the line was Princess Beatrice, who arrived in 1857.

The Queen asserted that she had been "extremely crushed and kept under and hardly dared say a word" when she was a child. Was she going to apply similar methods to her own children? One thing was certain: school was out of the question. There was too much frivolity about it, and she did not intend the royal blood to be corrupted.

In the early days, the Princess Royal and the Prince of Wales used to quarrel. She was exceptionally bright **for** her age; he used to stammer; and he became angry when she teased him about it. The Princess was her father's favourite, for he always admired intelligence. Edward was a source of anxiety, which was understandable. The upbringing of the heir to the throne was a big responsibility, and he was far less keen on his studies than his elder sister.

Stockmar said that the Queen and Prince Albert were too young to direct Edward's education: they needed advice. When the Bishop of Oxford was consulted, he said that "the great object in view is to make him the perfect man." No doubt. Lord Melbourne was less high-faluting. He told them not to worry too much. "It [education] may be able to do much," he said, "but it does not do as much as is expected from it. It may mould the character, but it rarely alters it."

Eventually, a team of tutors was employed – headed by an Old Etonian named Henry Birch, who was paid £800 a year. When he was older, Prince Edward went to both Oxford and Cambridge, but he was never allowed to live in college with the other young men. Throughout his youth, and even into middle age, he was afraid of both his parents. Although he had been christened Albert Edward, he refused to use the first name. There could only be one Albert, he said after his father's death, "who by universal consent is, I think, deservedly known by the name of Albert the Good."

In her later years, Queen Victoria was a fond and sometimes indulgent grandmother. With her own

Right Victoria with Princess Beatrice, her youngest daughter.

children, she was strict. She read history to them; gave them religious instruction; and listened to their prayers. As with so many other things in her life, the pattern had been set by Albert.

10 The Death of Albert

IT WAS ALL VERY WELL to appoint a commission to look into the sanitary conditions of the working classes, but Albert might have started closer to home. Main drainage had not been installed in Windsor Castle until the 1840s and, even then, parts of the premises were almost unusable. The trouble was the fearful smell which issued from the neighbouring cesspools. It was a nauseous invitation to catch that scourge of the nineteenth century – typhoid.

The Prince was nothing if not fastidious, and it seems strange that he ignored this problem. Hardly less mysterious was his readiness to employ Sir James Clark as the Royal physician. After the unhappy affair of Flora Hastings, Clark had received few patients, but the Queen loyally retained his services – and the Prince, apparently, did not object. Time had not sharpened the doctor's skill, and his diagnoses were as haphazard as ever.

Albert had been overworking; there was no doubt about that. The first signs that there might be something more seriously wrong with him appeared at the end of a wet day in November, 1861. The Prince had been inspecting some buildings for the new Royal Military Academy at Sandhurst. When he returned home, he complained of feeling unwell. The symptoms seemed to be rheumatism, insomnia, and a general feeling of depression.

Shortly afterwards, he paid a flying visit to Cambridge. The Prince of Wales, who was up at the University, had committed the blunder of falling in love with an actress. The affair had ended after a series of

"They are not fit to attend a sick cat." *Lord Clarendon on the Prince's doctors*

Above The Prince of Wales worried his parents because he preferred amusement to work. Here is is seen playing tennis at Baden-Baden, a health resort in Germany.

letters in that heavy style of righteousness of which the Prince Consort was such a master. The trip itself had been an errand of forgiveness. He felt calmer in mind when he returned to Windsor Castle, but his health was worse. Sir James Clark, with his talent for misreading symptoms, diagnosed a chill.

Next week, Albert became more and more depressed and he complained of increasing weakness. Nevertheless, he kept on working. His mind, like those of the nation's statesmen, was preoccupied with what became known as the "*Trent* Case."

The *Trent* was a British ship which had been sailing to England from Cuba during the early days of the American Civil War. On board were two envoys to England from the rebel Southern States. During the voyage, she was stopped and boarded by a Federal (Northern) warship, and all the male passengers were taken off her.

As Palmerston and Gladstone agreed, the idea of a British vessel being treated like this on the high seas was intolerable. Lord John Russell, the Foreign Secretary, was instructed to draft a dispatch which was also an ultimatum. The Northern States must release the captives at once, or Britain would declare war.

It was a tough document, and Albert doubted whether such strong language was advisable. Getting up at seven o'clock one morning, he rewrote the draft in more moderate terms. The Cabinet approved his version: war was avoided, and the envoys were released. It was one of Albert's more successful efforts.

But it had been difficult to compose. "I am so weak," he said, "that I can hardly hold the pen." Sir James Clark still insisted that there was nothing seriously the matter. The Prince did not agree with him. He was convinced that he would never recover. When the doctor was asked whether a second opinion might not be useful, he assured the Queen that there was no cause for alarm.

Eventually, it was Lord Palmerston who decided that the farce had gone on for long enough, and that a Dr. Watson should be consulted. Watson's verdict was immediate and positive. Prince Albert was suffering from typhoid fever. Had he been called in earlier, he might have been able to do something about it. Unfortunately, it was now too late.

The fever mounted: the Prince swung from delirium into consciousness and back into delirium. Sometimes he imagined he was back at Rosenau, wandering happily through the woods. At other times, he was peevishly in the present, demanding drinks of raspberry vinegar in seltzer water. Princess Alice played hymns on a piano in a neighbouring room. *Rock of Ages* was her father's favourite, and he asked for it again and again. The Queen read aloud to him from Sir Walter Scott's novel *Peveril of the Peak*. She and Clark were now the only people who believed in his chances of recovery. Princess Alice tried to convince her of the terrible truth, but she refused to believe it.

> "Oh! to be cut off in the prime of life – to see our pure, happy, quiet, domestic life, which *alone* enabled me to bear my *much* disliked position, CUT OFF at forty-two – when I *had* hoped with such instinctive certainty that God never *would* part us, and would let us grow old together – is *too awful*, **too cruel!**" *Victoria on the death of Albert*

Below Victoria and Albert together just before the Prince's last illness.

Above Prince Albert's hearse, with undertaker's mutes.

"With Prince Albert we have buried our sovereign. This German Prince has governed England for twenty-one years with a wisdom and energy such as none of our kings have ever shown." *Benjamin Disraeli*

On 14th December, the Prince Consort seemed to be better. Then he relapsed, and, at last, the reality of the situation became clear to the Queen. One by one, the royal children were assembled; and, one by one, they said good-bye to their father. At 10.45 on the evening of the 14th December, 1861, he died. The Queen let out a short, heart-rendering, cry of despair. The long evening of her own life had begun.

11 Years of Darkness

ALBERT HAD NEVER LIKED EMOTIONAL SCENES. He had been a man with an iron will: an intellectual who ruled his feelings with the calm precision of his mind. He had not, he once said, clung on to life; but, to Victoria, his life was the most precious thing in the world. During her long reign, most of her close friends died, but she shed no tears like those she shed for Albert. Her grief threw her into agonies until it seemed as if she would go mad. "My *life* as a *happy* one is ended!" wrote this broken widow of forty-two. "The world is gone for me."

Her life had, indeed, become a gradual process of withdrawal. The eager and excited girl who loved parties had faded out of the social scene under Albert's influence. Now, with the buttress of her life destroyed, she withdrew completely. One year of mourning faded into another, and the Queen's grief shows no signs of abating. A mantle of misery was thrown across the court, and the courtiers, understandably, grew restive. They were compelled to go about in dark clothes: balls and parties were forbidden, and it sometimes seemed to be a crime to smile. Even the clothing trade suffered from lack of orders for the customary finery of the well-to-do. Eventually the public began to wonder why so much money (£385,000 a year) was paid out to support a monarch who seemed to do so little.

But Victoria was determined to keep the pall of darkness intact. She insisted that, every night, Albert's bed should be turned down, and his clothes set out. Her own life would be his memorial, but there had to be something more tangible. How, best, could she honour her late and endlessly lamented husband?

"I am on a dreary sad pinnacle of solitary grandeur." *Victoria on widowhood*

"I am anxious to repeat *one* thing, and *that one* is my firm resolve, my *irrevocable decision*, viz., that *his* wishes – *his* plans – about everything are to be *my* law! And no *human power* will make me swerve from *what he* decided and wished." *Victoria on her attitude following Prince Albert's death*

He was buried at Frogmore near Windsor in a mausoleum which had been built at a cost of £200,000. There was a place beside him for herself; but there had to be something even more impressive, and certainly less private. An early thought was that a huge granite obelisk should be erected in London. It transpired, however, that no British quarry could yield a large enough piece. In the end, she approved an idea of building a memorial hall with a statue near its entrance. The cost would be provided from public subscriptions.

Unfortunately, the public's grief was less than the Queen's. Only £60,000 was subscribed, which was enough for the statue but not for the hall. Another appeal was made, which produced £10,000, and Parliament agreed to chip in with £50,000. From these amounts, a joint stock company was formed, and the Albert Hall in London was built as a private speculation.

An architect named Sir Gilbert Scott was commissioned to design the statue. He was an artist who specialized in the Gothic, or English Medieval, which had taken over from the calm, elegant Georgian as the fashionable style. Much of his work had been devoted to restoring cathedrals; he also built St. Pancras railway station to look as much like one of these venerable and elaborate buildings as possible. He had won several gold medals, and he was known to be very reliable. There were even some who suggested that he was chosen for his hard work rather than for his ability.

The Queen wanted the statue to be built as near as possible to the site of the Great Exhibition in Hyde Park. A plot of land was chosen in Kensington Gardens, and Sir Gilbert went to work. Prince Albert was depicted with the exhibition catalogue in his hand, surrounded by pillars and pinnacles bearing carvings of great achievements in the arts and sciences: the very epitome of the pomp and solidity of Victorian ideals. The Albert Hall was built opposite on the site of Gore House to the design of two officers in the Royal Engineers. When it was completed, it provided seats for 8,000 within its colossal 735-feet circumference.

Left The Albert Memorial, Kensington Gore, London.

Elsewhere in the country, there were lesser monuments to Albert – such as a stone at Balmoral to mark the place where he shot his last stag, and another at Windsor to immortalize his final foray after pheasants.

But the country was becoming impatient. In March, 1864, when the Queen still showed no signs of being about to come out of her seclusion at Windsor, a wag put up a poster outside Buckingham Palace. "These commanding premises to be let or sold," it announced, "in consequence of the late occupant's declining business."

Eventually, Her Majesty decided that the time had come to explain the situation. As a medium, she chose the columns of *The Times*. The item appeared under the heading of "The Court" in the issue dated 6th April, 1864. Although it was unsigned, the prose style left readers in no doubt about the authorship. It was, so far as is known, the only instance of a reigning British monarch contributing to a daily newspaper:

"The Queen heartily appreciates the desire of her subjects to see her, and whatever she *can* do to gratify them in this loyal and affectionate wish, she *will* do. Whenever any real object is to be attained by her appearing on public occasions, any national interest to be promoted, or anything to be encouraged which is for the good of her people, Her Majesty will not shrink from any personal sacrifice or exertion, however painful.

"But there are other and higher duties than those of mere representation which are now thrown upon the Queen, alone and unassisted – duties which she cannot neglect without injury to the public service, which weight unceasingly upon her, overwhelming her with work and anxiety.

"The Queen has laboured conscientiously to discharge these duties till her health and strength, already shaken by the utter and everabiding desolation which has taken the place of her former happiness, have been seriously impaired.

"To call upon her to undergo, in addition, the fatigue of those mere state ceremonies which can be equally well

Above Britannia's Valentine, a *Punch* cartoon suggesting that the Queen should appear in public rather more often.

"From the hour she gets out of bed till she gets into it again there is work, work, work – letter boxes, questions, etc., which are dreadfully exhausting – and if she had not comparative rest and quiet in the evening she would most likely not be *alive*. Her brain is constantly overtaxed." *Victoria about herself – in a letter written in 1863*

performed by other members of her family is to ask her to run the risk of entirely disabling herself for the discharge of those other duties which cannot be neglected without serious injury to the public interests.

"The Queen will, however, do what she can – in the manner least trying to her health, strength, and spirits – to meet the loyal wishes of her subjects, to afford that support and countenance to society, and to give that encouragement to trade which is desired of her. More the Queen cannot do; and more the kindness and good feeling of her people will surely not exact from her."

Albert, with his prodigious industry, had taken much of the burden of state from Victoria. It was, perhaps, proof of his effectiveness that she could find time for nine pregnancies *and* the duties of Queen of England. With Albert gone, she was confronted by the daunting prospect of making decisions on her own – and by the

> "Her Majesty's loyal subjects will be very pleased to hear that their Sovereign is about to break her protracted seclusion."
> The Times *1st April, 1864*

scarcely less difficult one of seeing that they were carried out.

She had, in fact, already made up her mind to continue in the manner that she believed Albert would have done: to carry on his plans and wishes, and to permit nobody to lead her or to dictate to her. Although she does not seem to have realized it, the last two sentiments were hopeless. The Queen was bound to be led, for the nature of sovereignty had been changing. "Reform" was the war cry of the nineteenth century. It echoed off the walls of the corridors of power, and it was fired like a cannon ball from the mouths of radicals who thundered their beliefs from platforms in Mechanics' Institutes throughout the country. It affected the lot of the working man; it affected Parliament; it affected the monarch. The Queen's ancestors had a considerable say in the running of the country, but times had changed. Now, political parties were better organized, and Cabinets were no longer chosen in the old informal manner – if the Liberals were elected to power, it was no use for Victoria to say that she disliked their leaders. More people than the five per cent who had been allowed the vote since 1832 were demanding a say in government, and when, in 1867, they achieved this, they expected Parliament to take some notice of the way they thought. Ministers, who would have to stand for re-election, insisted on doing what they and the voters wanted without interference. Against many of her inclinations, this opiniated and very voluble woman had to watch the nation's policies being determined by her Cabinets.

As Walter Bagehot, the historian, was to write, "The Sovereign has, under a constitutional monarchy such as ours, three rights – the right to be consulted, the right to encourage, the right to rule." To the discomfort of her ministers, Queen Victoria wanted more. She desired the right to dictate.

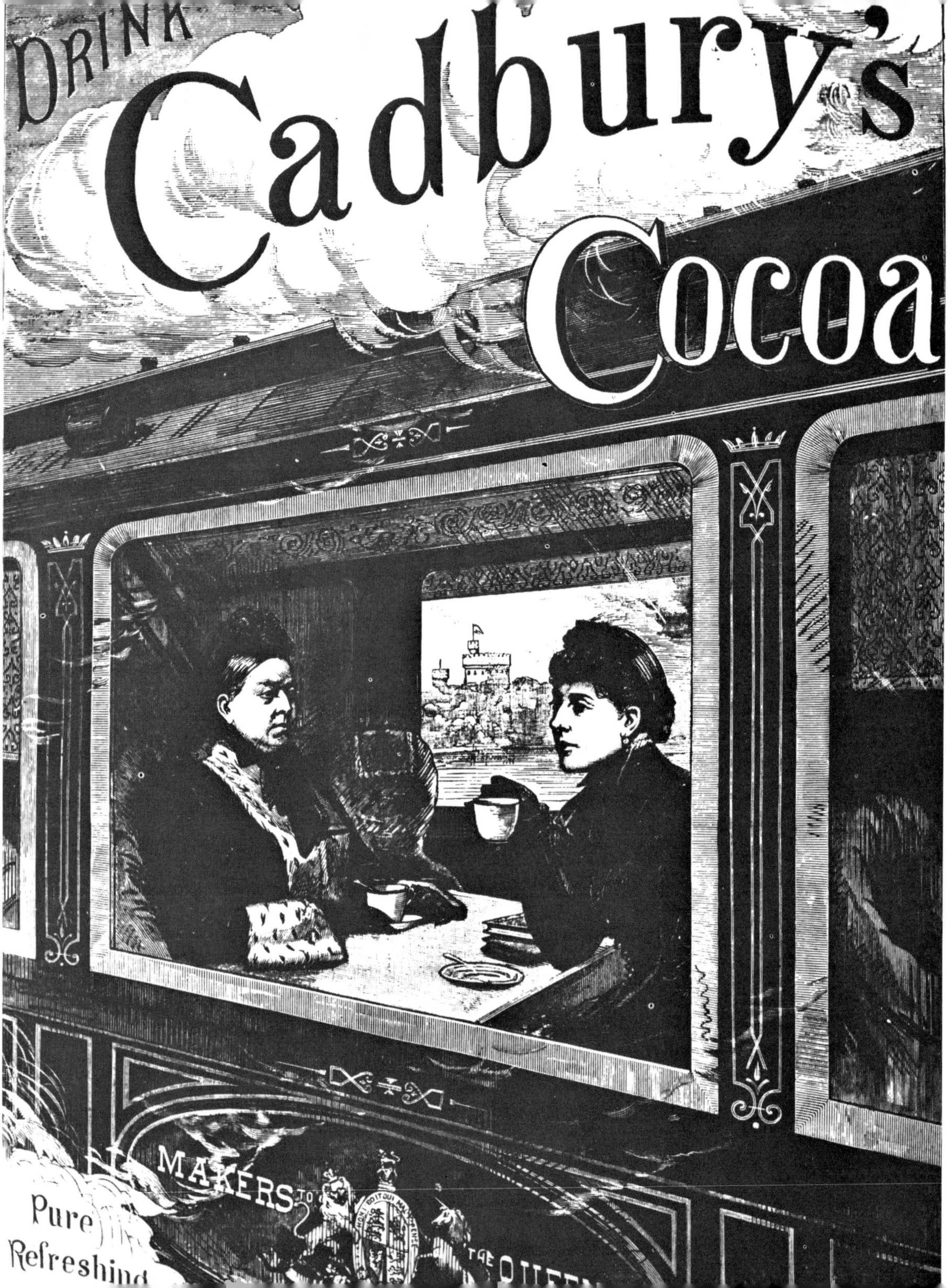

DRINK
Cadbury's
Cocoa
MAKERS TO THE QUEEN
Pure
Refreshing

12 The Opinions of a Queen

WHATEVER THE REST OF THE NATION may have thought, the Queen's ministers knew that she still wanted to be active in affairs of state. For the first few weeks of mourning, she had refused to see them; but, once she had decided to model the rest of her life on Albert's, her enthusiasm for government returned. Unfortunately for their peace of mind, she often opposed them on matters of foreign policy.

The first conflict to arouse her interest concerned the future of Schleswig-Holstein. In 1864 both Denmark and Prussia were laying claim to this pocket state on the border between them, and the situation was nothing if not confusing. As Lord Palmerston said, "only three people have ever really understood the Schleswig-Holstein question – the Prince Consort, who is dead – a German professor, who has gone mad – and I, who have forgotten all about it."

Her Majesty took Prussia's side for the simple reason that Albert had always taken Prussia's side. Palmerston and Lord John Russell, on the other hand, favoured Denmark, for the very good reason that Prussia was becoming ever wealthier and stronger. If its growth were to upset the balance of power and cause a conflict with France or Austria, then Britain too might have to go to war. In the end, nobody did anything at all about it, and Prussia was left to wage a brief war against Denmark without any hindrance from the United Kingdom. It was, in a way, a victory for Victoria as well as for Prussia.

In 1866, however, she decided that she had been mistaken about Prussia. When the Seven Weeks War

> "In the midst of so much wealth, there seems to be nothing but ruin. As far as the eye can reach, one sees nothing but chimneys, flaming furnaces . . . with wretched cottages around them . . . Add to this a thick and black atmosphere . . . and you have but a faint impression of the life . . . which a third of a million of my poor subjects are forced to lead." *Victoria, after a visit to the Black Country*

erupted between that country and Austria, she was in favour of supporting Austria. She pleaded with her ministers – and, again, the nation did nothing about it. Round two went to Lord Palmerston.

In home affairs. the Queen's views were a mass of contradictions. She had supported Albert's move to make duelling illegal, and she detested public executions (the last one took place in 1868). On the other hand, when the Ten Hour Bill was introduced in 1847, she opposed it. The idea was to limit the working hours of women and children employed in mills and factories. The employers bewailed the fact that, if it were passed, it would cost them seven working weeks per child per year. Victoria might have supported this measure, which, since men could do little without their child helpers, would have reduced everyone's hours of work. However she allowed her humanitarian feeling to be overcome by her fear that the Liberal government, which included many factory-owners, would be split by the Bill.

Ireland bothered her enormously, and she often expressed a wish to visit that stricken country where the peasants, most of them Catholics, suffered poverty all the time, and famine for much of it. Although, as Queen of England, she was also head of the Anglican Church, she supported plans to increase the grant to an Irish training college for Roman Catholic priests. An educated clergy in a priest-ridden country would, she believed, be an advantage – and, in any case, she loathed the bigoted opinions of the Protestants. "I blush for the form of religion we profess, that it should be so void of all right feelings, and so wanting in Charity," she wrote.

She didn't see why Ireland should be treated differently from the rest of the country. Government by troops was terrible, and it was wretchedly cruel of landlords to evict the peasantry. English tenants were treated better – though she seems to have ignored the unpardonable excesses of the Highland lairds, who were busy clearing away crofters to make way for sheep

Above Belfast police charge against Protestant rioters who opposed Gladstone's policy of Home Rule for Ireland.

and grouse-shooting.

She certainly had no intention of allowing the Irish to govern themselves. When, in 1881, the leading protagonist of Home Rule, Charles Stewart Parnell, was arrested for encouraging the peasants to refuse to pay rent, she thought it "a great thing." She disapproved of Parnell's private life – he was accused of adultery as co-respondent in a famous divorce case – and she was shocked by what she learned of the crimes of his Land League from reading police reports. Her verdict "Gladstone's most fatal move" when Parnell was released in 1882 was perhaps unreasonably prejudiced: certainly some way had to be found of meeting the demands of the Irish people, though few Englishmen wanted to go as far as Gladstone did towards giving them

> **"It is worth being shot at – to see how much one is loved."**
> *Victoria, after a mentally retarded youth named Roderick McLean had fired a pistol at her*

Above Victoria receives Nasr-ed-Din, Shah of Persia, during his state visit to England in 1873.

Home Rule. The Queen became more and more hostile to the Liberals, who by their repeated demands for reform seemed to be suggesting that her country was something less than perfect. It was only because Mr. Gladstone himself was tough enough to stand up to her that the party was able to govern at all.

Victoria's views on most things were flexible and, often, unpredictable. She did not bring strong political opinions to her interference in government – but she was a woman who had great faith in her judgement and a powerful desire to have her own way.

13 Dear Mr. Disraeli

VICTORIA COULD NEVER really have modelled herself on Albert. The actions of the Prince Consort were motivated by his reason. His wife's sprang from her heart.

The Queen had first met Benjamin Disraeli in 1845; but the rising Tory politician, who was already a successful novelist, does not seem to have made much impression on her. Nor, come to that, did William Ewart Gladstone, with whom she also became acquainted that year. But, then, Mr. Gladstone never succeeded in impressing the monarch. With Disraeli, it was a very different matter.

It was some years after the death of Prince Albert that this handsome statesman, with his eyeglass dangling from his neck and an orchid in his buttonhole, first came to her notice. In 1866, he had been appointed Chancellor of the Exchequer: two years later, he became Prime Minister. But his ascent to political fame was not what won the Queen's favour. It was, predictably, his veneration of Albert.

Disraeli had supported the Parliamentary grant which made possible the Albert Memorial. In his conversation, he enthused over the Prince Consort's fine qualities – and, when he cared to, Mr. Disraeli could enthuse very eloquently indeed. For her part, the Queen presented him with a copy of her late husband's speeches bound in white Morocco leather, and the strands of friendship became pleasantly woven.

As is the case of most relationships, timing had a good deal to do with it. If Disraeli's glamour had been forced to compete with Albert's earnestness, things might have been different. If his coming to power had

> "The Prince is the only person whom Mr. Disraeli has ever known who realized the Ideal. None with whom he is acquainted have ever approached it." *Disraeli, writing to the Queen about her late husband*

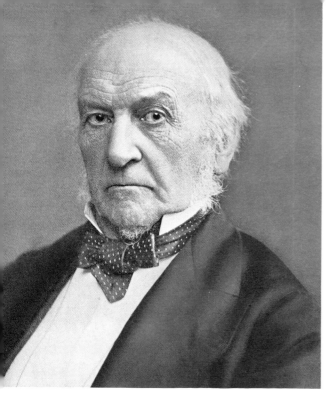

Above left William Ewart Gladstone, and *right*, Benjamin Disraeli, Earl of Beaconsfield.

"The Almighty seems to sustain and spare me for some purpose of His own, deeply unworthy as I know myself to be." *Gladstone, on hearing that he had become Prime Minister*

occurred a year or two earlier, Victoria might still have been unimpressed. But now the wound of widowhood, though never healed, was at last becoming bearable. In 1866, Victoria announced her intention of opening Parliament herself for the first time since Albert's death. She was determined to go through with it. Even the death of her beloved uncle, King Leopold, at the end of 1865, did not weaken her resolution.

At last, the Queen had stepped out of the dark corridor of mourning, and, within two years, there was Mr. Disraeli to guide her through the patchy sunshine of government. He did it so beautifully. He had such charm and humour, and his respect was never too humble. He did not order her about in the manner of her other confidant, John Brown – the towering Highland ghillie who had become her friend and personal servant. Nor did he conduct himself with the ponderous reverence of Mr. Gladstone. Disraeli was a magnificent judge of manners, and he knew just the right attitude to employ.

He gave her a complete set of his novels; and when, in 1868, Victoria's own *Leaves from the Journal of Our Life in the Highlands* was published, he waggishly spoke of "we authors, Ma'am." What was more to the point, perhaps, was that he sent her frequent and amusing letters about affairs of state. At last the Queen felt that she knew *everything*.

Victoria revelled in this new companionship. She sent him bunches of spring flowers which she and her ladies had picked at Osborne, and she took the trouble to find out that he liked the primroses best. She had only one care in the world, and that was that the Government might be overthrown. It was just like the days of Lord Melbourne.

The Queen's fears were justified. Disraeli, hoping for popularity, introduced a Reform Bill that gave the vote to many more small tradesmen and workers. But it had always been the Liberals who had campaigned for reform in the past, and the new voters were not fooled by the Tories' sudden conversion. Within nine months of taking office, Disraeli and his Conservatives were thrown out, and Gladstone and the Liberals came in. The Queen, again, felt lost. There were so many

> "You may tell the French engineer that if he can accomplish it I will give him my blessing in my own name, and in the name of all the ladies of England." *Victoria, on the Channel Tunnel Project*

Below John Brown, Victoria's Highland ghillie, with the Queen and some of her grandchildren at Osborne in 1870.

problems: the Irish land system, the organization of the fighting services, education, justice, the question of whether sailors in the Navy should be allowed to grow beards, and so on. She felt powerless – if only Albert were alive!

Gladstone's solemn manner did little to help. She tried to like him; but the man would persist, as she put it, in speaking "to Me as if I was a public meeting." When the Liberal Prime Minister decreed that the Commander-in-Chief of the Army should be responsible to Parliament and not to the sovereign, she was mortified. It seemed like a personal attack on Albert's memory. And when he abolished the purchase of commissions in the Army, which had caused disaster in the Crimean War, few officers having even served with their regiments before, she joined with the House of Lords in opposing it. Again, she was powerless, unless she wanted to cause a constitutional crisis. She was learning an uncomfortable lesson on the new rights of monarchy.

Gladstone put into effect a series of useful reforms: the secret ballot at elections, a tidying-up of the law on trade unions, and above all, the creation of a national system of compulsory primary education. It was not these that upset the Queen so much, but the desperately serious way in which the Prime Minister treated his work. He ignored the claims of tradition, he was careless of the courtly graces, and he never allowed personalities to interfere with politics.

But all bad things come to an end. In 1874, the Liberals went out of office, deserted by the country because they had raised the income tax and imposed licensing hours on public houses. Dear Mr. Disraeli was back. The spring flowers on the Isle of Wight were ready for picking, and the Prime Minister received more than his fair share of primroses. Three years later, he proposed that Her Majesty should assume the title of Empress of India. She was delighted and, in return, conferred on him the title of Earl of Beaconsfield. To celebrate, they dined together at Windsor Castle. The Queen wore a dazzling display of jewels that had been sent to her by

Below Victoria visits Disraeli at his Buckinghamshire home in 1877, the first time a Prime Minister had been so honoured since Sir Robert Peel.

the Indian Rajahs.

Queen Victoria took great interest in India. The keeper of the museum at Lahore, John Lockwood Kipling (Rudyard Kipling's father), was instructed to decorate a "Durbar Room" at Osborne. It was a continuing reminder of her dominion beyond the seas. When Lord Salisbury referred to Indians as "black men" he was made to apologize; and she attempted to save a rebel leader from the gallows after he had killed some white people. She was unsuccessful – though it served to remind people of her leniency after the Indian Mutiny. She had blamed the massacre on misgovernment by the East India Company, and had insisted that there should be no victimization. She herself was almost universally adored by the peoples of the Empire, however much they loathed some aspects of British rule.

Disraeli continued to charm her. As he once said to Matthew Arnold, the poet, "You have heard me called a flatterer, and it is true. Everybody likes flattery, and when you come to royalty you should lay it on with a trowel."

It was, of course, a considerable misrepresentation of his own value. He did everything so charmingly, but at least he did everything. When he purchased the Suez Canal shares in 1875, he pulled off a shrewd financial coup, strengthening Britain's position in the troubled Middle East. But he made it appear as if he had done it especially to please the Queen. He told her everything that happened at cabinet meetings – even reporting what individual ministers had said. The practice horrified Mr. Gladstone, but Victoria loved it. In Disraeli's presence, they said, this short, stout, rather plain and ageing woman "came out like a flower." He was more than the nation's Prime Minister: he was as good for the Queen.

Above The Prince of Wales in India, 1875.

"It is just settled; you have it, Madam . . . Four millions sterling! and almost immediately. There was only one firm that could do it – Rothschilds. They behaved admirably; advanced the money at a low rate, and the entire interest of the Khedive is now yours, Madam." *Disraeli reporting to the Queen on the purchase of the Suez Canal shares*

14 Russian Roulette

DISRAELI HAD TOLD THE QUEEN that she had a right, if she so desired, to dismiss the entire cabinet. This was true in theory, but she would have found it hard to assemble enough loyal politicans to form another one. The fate of Charles I still stood as a frightening reminder to monarchs who might go too far. She never put her powers to the test, but she did once foil an attempt by the "really wicked" Mr. Gladstone to include in his ministry a man who had offended her. His name was Henry Labouchère; and he owned a newspaper named *Truth*, which was constantly making jokes at the expense of royalty. However, Victoria had discovered that Labouchère had lived with his wife before marrying her. Thus she was able to base her objection on moral rather than political grounds.

She would only accept him, she said, if he cut himself off from *Truth* – and if, in view of what she conceived as his murky past, he took a post in which he never need meet her. Labouchère refused the conditions, and turned the guns of his newspaper on to her by suggesting that Buckingham Palace should become a home for "fallen women." In the unpredictable manner of popular opinion, this served to win sympathy for the Queen.

The Queen felt safe with Disraeli: she trusted him as she never trusted Gladstone. On one occasion, however, their pleasantly relaxed relationship underwent a severe test. The year was 1877: Russia and Turkey were once again at each other's throats, and if the Russians won they might soon challenge the Royal Navy's control of the Mediterranean. Was this to be another Crimean

A paper fleet they say is ours
If what we hear is true.
Let's hope the fleets of other
   powers
Are stationary too.
Verse by Wilfred Lawson, M.P., after the despatch of the British fleet to Constantinople by W. H. Smith, First Lord of the Admiralty (and the man who started station bookstalls)

War? Victoria wanted war, certainly. As she wrote in her journal: "Oh, if the Queen were a man, she would like to go and give those Russians, whose word one cannot believe, such a hiding!"

On the music hall stage, a singer echoed her opinion with the song:

We don't want to fight, but, by jingo if we do,
We've got the ships, we've got the men, we've got the
money, too.
We've fought the Bear before, and while Britons
shall be true,
The Russians shall not have Constantinople.

But by no means everybody agreed. To her disgust, she learned that an anti-Turkish meeting had been held in London. The Duke of Westminster had presided, and Mr. Gladstone had been present. She felt that the Attorney-General should hear about it, for "it can't be constitutional." It was, of course. Indeed many of the public supported Mr. Gladstone, in spite of their dislike of the Russians, when they heard of the horrible tortures

Left Victoria passes along Hackney Road, Bethnal Green, during a visit to the poor areas of the East End of London.

that the Turkish *bashi-bazouks* had used against rebel Bulgarian prisoners.

Disraeli was playing a cautious, even subtle, game, which the Queen interpreted as a sign of weakness. Telegrams and memoranda from the palace piled up on the Prime Minister's desk. In one of them, she wrote: "The Queen is feeling terribly anxious lest delay should cause us to be too late and lose our prestige for ever! It worries her day and night."

At one point, she threatened to abdicate rather than "kiss Russia's feet." The Prime Minister sent the fleet to Gallipoli, but that was not enough, and the royal out-pourings continued. Fortunately not many people knew of them, certainly not the Russian Ambassador in London. In a dispatch to St. Petersburg, he referred to "this conspiracy of a half-mad woman with a political clown."

The Queen was not half-mad, and Disraeli was no clown. His clever manipulation of the situation resulted in the Congress of Berlin of 1878. Otto von Bismarck, the Chancellor of Germany, took the chair, and managed the proceedings with considerable skill. Peace with honour was assured. Cyprus was given to Britain – on condition that the nation paid an annual tribute to the Sultan, and pledged itself to protect Asia Minor. An unfortunate result was that Germany became stronger; but for the moment, with France a republic and the Austrian Emperor on bad terms with all his fellow-sovereigns, the Empire ruled by her eldest daughter's father-in-law was Victoria's favourite great power.

When the Prime Minister came back to Downing Street from Berlin, he found a bouquet of flowers from the Queen waiting for him. As for Her Majesty, the successful outcome caused her to bury the last shreds of mourning. For the first time for eighteen years, she attended a ball – and actually took to the dance floor and waltzed.

"Dizzy," as she called the Prime Minister, had done it again. He and the Foreign Secretary were rewarded with the Order of the Garter.

"An undersized creature almost as broad as she was long. She looked like a cook, had a bluish-red face and was more or less mentally deranged." *Otto von Bismarck, Chancellor of Germany, on Queen Victoria.*

"Ministers are getting rapidly reconciled to keeping her well away and in point of fact enjoy the outward appearance of having all the power in their own hands." *Sir Henry Ponsonby, the Queen's private secretary*

Opposite Bismarck visits Disraeli at the Kaiserhof Hotel during the negotiations which led to the Congress of Berlin.

15 The Queen in Conflict

IN 1881, DISRAELI DIED – his sickbed swathed in freshly picked primroses from Osborne. Mr. Gladstone, on the other hand, was far from dead. He was four years younger than his Tory rival, and his political energies showed no signs of flagging. In the previous year, he had taken over the ship of state on what was to be one of the stormiest voyages of his career.

The Queen and Gladstone were as far apart as any two people could be. The former was emotional, sometimes capricious, and always eager to pour out her thoughts in torrents of swirling prose. When Mr. Gladstone wished to let off steam, he silently chopped wood.

There can be few better examples of this clash of temperament than their attitudes to the plight of General Gordon. Gordon, like the Queen, was a romantic, and his final defeat at Khartoum was largely of his own making. When in 1885 he left England for the Soudan, where the Mahdi had led the people in revolt against the English-backed Egyptian government, his instructions had been to report on the situation out there – nothing more. The fact that he remained there, and held off the hostile Dervishes for a year, was his own decision. Gordon believed that it was essential to hold Khartoum. The British Government was less certain.

It may have been a brave action, but it was unrealistic. The greater part of the Soudan was occupied by the Dervishes. Gordon had only a handful of badly-trained troops. When the situation became desperate, public opinion in England demanded a relief expedition. The Queen, reflecting the will of her people, demanded it

"The downfall of Beaconsfield-ism is like the vanishing of some vast magnificent castle in an Italian romance. It is too big, however, to be all taken in at once. Meantime, while I inwardly rejoice, I am against all outward signs of exultation, for they are not chivalrous, and would tend to barbarise political warfare. We may be well content to thank God in silence. But the outlook is tremendous" *Gladstone writing to the Duke of Argyll after winning the election of 1880*

Opposite top Roderick Maclean is pounced on by Eton boys after firing a revolver at Victoria in 1882.

Centre Socialist rioters dash off from Trafalgar Square to loot fashionable shops in St. James', in 1886.

Bottom Police search for weapons at Tralee Station, Ireland, in 1886.

> "To think of your dear, noble, heroic brother, who served his Country and his Queen so truly, so heroically, with a self-sacrifice so edifying to the World, not having been rescued. That the promises of support were not fulfilled which I so frequently and constantly pressed on those who asked him to go – is to me grief *inexpressible!* Indeed, it has made me ill."
>
> *The Queen writing to General Gordon's sister*

Below An early Madame Tussaud's waxwork showing the death of General Gordon.

too. She trembled, she wrote to Gladstone, "for Gen. Gordon's safety. If anything befalls *him*, the result will be awful."

Gladstone was unmoved. He delayed the departure of the relief force until it was too late. Khartoum fell to the Dervishes, and Gordon was killed – leaving the Prime Minister, it seemed, with little on his conscience. Queen Victoria, on the other hand, was moved to tears.

Mr. Gladstone had other matters to occupy his more objective mind. The question of home rule for Ireland, that ever-recurring problem of British politicians, was coming relentlessly to the boil. To be fair to the Liberal Prime Minister, his plans were not unreasonable. He believed that the landowners, who had been responsible for so much of the country's misery, should be forced to sell their estates to the government – and that a local parliament should be set up in Dublin to deal with Irish affairs.

The Queen was against it. Moderate as these measures may now seem to be, she disliked the idea of losing control of any member of the Imperial family of nations. As in many things, she did not allow lack of knowledge to stop her from interfering. The Home Rule Bill would have to be thrown out – and with it, hopefully, Mr. Gladstone.

Her actions in the great crisis that came to a head in 1886 were, to say the least, unconstitutional. The sovereign's duty is to support the country's elected government. In this instance, however, Victoria cheerfully went behind her Prime Minister's back, and conspired with the opposition leader, Lord Salisbury. She even showed Salisbury letters which had passed between herself and the Cabinet, and asked him for advice. Nothing, it seemed, was barred in her efforts to ensure that the Bill was defeated.

She – or, perhaps one should say, Lord Salisbury, the leader of the opposition – was successful. Indeed, his lordship's arguments against Home Rule were so persuasive that the party divisions, unchanged since Peel had left the Tories forty years before, were again

Left Gladstone and his Home Rule Bill are kicked out in 1886. Lord Salisbury wears the shovel hat, Joseph Chamberlain the monocle and check trousers.

thrown into chaos. After an angry debate in the Commons, Joseph Chamberlain, the Birmingham screw-manufacturer and radical M.P., was seen to rise from the Liberal benches, and cross the floor of the House. Like the other rebels who followed him, Mr. Chamberlain was a staunch "man of the people," who was bitterly opposed to Tory policy in general. But there was a point beyond which he and his colleagues were not prepared to go. They all believed fervently in the Empire – so much so, that they were not prepared to lose even such an uncomfortable fragment as Ireland.

The unlikeable Mr. Gladstone and his proposals were overthrown: the more endearing Lord Salisbury came

"Already six months of the year passed! How terribly time flies! and in what awful times we live! Ireland no better . . . Egypt in a dreadful state – the Sultan unmanageable and the other Powers behaving very ill!! God help and guide me! – a very fine day." *Victoria on 18th June, 1882*

to power. Victoria said that she "could not help feeling relieved, and think it best for the interests of the country."

The British Empire, in Africa and India, was growing in size and in wealth. In 1897, the nation was given a chance to study those significant red blobs on the map, when the Indian and Colonial Exhibition was held at South Kensington. Lord Rosebery, who had briefly been Liberal Prime Minister, suggested that the Queen should wear her crown for the opening ceremony, but she refused. This was partly a vestige of her mourning for Albert (as a sign of her widowhood, she would not wear a crown out-of-doors), and partly a symbol of her attitude to the Empire. She may have been an imperialist; but, as she saw it, she was the mother and the colonies were her children.

Alas – the expanding Empire was not quite so healthy as the Queen liked to believe. As if Ireland were not sickness enough, there was the problem of South Africa. Victoria disliked the Boers who, since 1883, had been governing themselves in the Transvaal under President Paul Kruger. She considered them "a most merciless and cruel neighbour." When Dr. Jameson made his famous raid on the Transvaal in 1896, she was distressed at its failure – and enraged at the conduct of her grandson, Kaiser Wilhelm II of Germany, who sent a telegram of congratulations to Kruger.

Below A family party at Osborne in 1898, with the future Kings George V (bearded), Edward VIII (third from left) and George VI (in front of his father).

16 Reunion with Prince Albert

ALTHOUGH SHE WAS STILL ACTIVELY INVOLVED in affairs of state, nobody could deny that the Queen was getting older. Her eyesight was beginning to fail, and she once misread a telegram announcing another defeat in South Africa as if it carried news of a victory. But if she needed comfort, she had only to go out into the streets. As she aged, so did Victoria's popularity with her people seem to swell.

The Prince of Wales was moving through middle age without, it seemed, any great awareness of his future responsibilities. There had even been talk of scandals. In an attempt to guide him towards the paths of duty and morality, Victoria asked *The Times* editor, John Delane, to publish frequent leading articles "pointing out the *immense* danger and evil of the wretched frivolity and levity of the views and lives of the Higher Classes." Delane obliged with just such a piece, but it had little effect.

In June 1887, she had celebrated the Golden Jubilee of her reign by driving to Westminster Abbey. She felt "very tired, but very happy." All her sons and daughters were married, and there were frequent visits by grand-children to Osborne. They loved to play in the Swiss Cottage, which Prince Albert had imported for the education of his own youngsters (it contained a full set of tools and cooking implements), and in the small fort he had built. Towards the end of her life, there were thirty-seven of them. They included the future Kaiser of Germany, the future King of Greece, the future King George V of Britain, the future Queen Maud of Norway, and the future King of Rumania. For the

time being, however, they were just children who adored their grandmother. As for Victoria, she doted on all of them.

Her every day was mapped out according to a strict timetable: indeed, the one unpardonable sin at court seemed to be lateness. She often went to the theatre, and enjoyed the performance of Henry Irving (whom she made the first knight of the British stage) and the Savoy Operas of W. S. Gilbert and Arthur Sullivan. She liked a play to have a good plot. Farce – provided the jokes were not too subtle, and there was no bawdiness – always made her laugh; and she adored the poetic works of Alfred Lord Tennyson. She read a great deal of fiction, too – though Albert would not have approved her taste in authors. She found George Eliot heavy going, and preferred popular romances.

On Tuesday, 22nd June, 1897, London awoke to one of the most colourful days in the capital's history. The occasion was Queen Victoria's Diamond Jubilee – or, as it was more commonly called, "Queen's Day." Throughout the country, there were celebrations – and the souvenir industry, an offshoot of the massproduction which became possible in the Victorian age, did a thriving trade. In almost every shop, or so it seemed, there were mugs and plates and picture postcards on sale – every one of them dedicated to the commemoration of sixty glorious years.

But London was the magnet which drew enormous crowds to watch the jubilee procession to St. Paul's Cathedral. It was, to say the least, a most sumptuous display of pomp and ceremony. The royal procession was headed by a captain ("of splendid height," the *Illustrated London News* reporter noted) and four troopers from the 2nd Life Guards. They were followed by six naval guns and their crews: by detachments from the Royal Horse Artillery, the Hussars and the Lancers. The Duke of Westminster, as Lord Lieutenant of London, rode on horseback accompanied by three volunteer officers. General Lord Roberts was mounted on a white Arab charger. There were soldiers from the

"Her court was pure; her life serene;
God gave her peace; her land reposed;
A thousand claims to reverence closed
In her as Mother, Wife and Queen."
First verse of a poem by Alfred, Lord Tennyson, paying homage to Victoria

Below Messrs. Pears, the soap manufacturers, illuminated their Oxford Street office in honour of Victoria's Golden Jubilee.

Opposite Victoria, Edward VII, George V and Edward VIII in 1900. George was a family man who didn't share his father's taste for a gay social life.

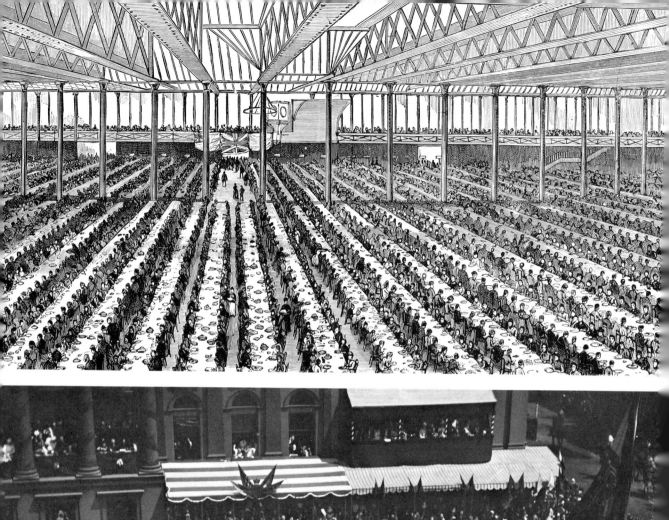
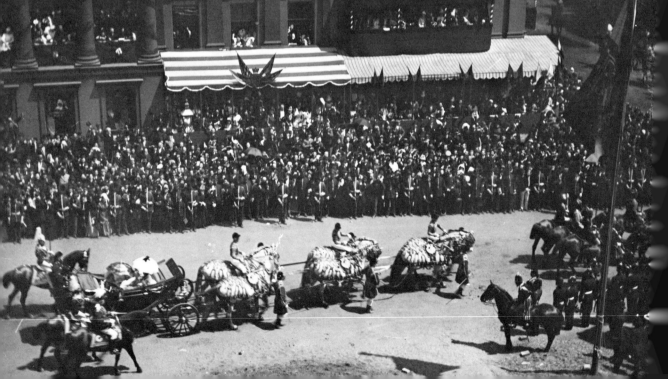

colonies, foreign envoys, and a host of equerries; and a large collection of royalty from overseas.

The Queen's carriage was drawn by eight gaily caparisoned cream horses. Her sons the Dukes of Edinburgh and Connaught sat on the dickey; the Prince of Wales rode behind. She was wearing a black dress, with the front empannelled in pigeon grey silk. On top of this, there was a mass of fine silvery embroidery carefully designed to include the rose, the shamrock and the thistle. Her cape was of black chiffon bedecked with white lace and silver embroidery, and her bonnet (in the words of a correspondent) "was richly wrought with jet and silver, and trimmed with white acacia and white ostrich feathers." In her small and still podgy hand, she carried a white silk sunshade.

Presently, the procession reached St. Paul's. To save the Queen the exertion of going inside, the bishops and priests conducted the service from the steps, while she remained in her carriage. Afterwards, she drove back to Buckingham Palace by way of the City.

After dark, there were illuminations and fireworks. The front of the Mansion House was lit by thousands of gas lamps, and the outline of the Star of India blazed colourfully from the roof. There had, the citizens of Britain agreed, never been a day like it. "From my heart I thank my beloved people," the Queen had told them in a message issued that morning. "May God Bless them." The poet Cosmo Monkhouse expressed the spirit of the people's reply:

Light of our Isles by day and night to us,
Kind as the Sun and steadfast as a star,
Victoria our Queen, victorious in Peace and War.

. . . and so on. There were several more verses.

When she was at Windsor, she went daily to the mausoleum at Frogmore. Albert's clothing was still laid out on his bed every evening, and water was put into his wash basin. The room had not changed since the evening of his death, but his ghost no longer haunted Victoria. The love remained, but the grief had gone.

On preceding pages
Left The Golden Jubilee in 1887 – *top*, six thousand poor people of Edinburgh are entertained to dinner under one roof, and *bottom*, the procession in London.

Right The Diamond Jubilee of 1897 – *top*, the procession in Mansion House Street, and *bottom*, Victoria with the Dukes and Duchesses of Edinburgh and Connaught. (*See also jacket picture*).

She had always been a great collector, and nothing was ever thrown away. Now she insisted that every object must be photographed, and the pictures stuck into carefully annotated albums. It was a task which never seemed to end; but, for Victoria, it was a way of re-living her life.

Public duties were still expected of her, and she spent a good deal of time opening exhibitions and laying foundation stones. When the Boer War at last broke out, in 1899, she gave up her annual visit to the South of France and, instead, visited Dublin. It was from there that a great part of the Army was recruited, and she considered this the least she could do to help

But she was becoming tired. Her memory was unreliable and her sight was dimmed by a cataract.

Below Victoria presents medals to heroes of colonial wars.

Nevertheless when, on the 14th January, 1901, Lord Roberts came to see her at Osborne after his victories in South Africa, she was well aware of what was going on, and she asked some penetrating questions. When the General had gone, however, she collapsed.

Just over a week later, on the 22nd January, she died. The Prince of Wales sent the following message at 6.45 in the afternoon:

My beloved mother the Queen has just (6.30) passed away, surrounded by her children and grandchildren.
(signed) Albert Edward.

It was a dismal, drizzly, night with no stars in the sky, and an atmosphere of gloom everywhere. People went indoors and drew their blinds. Out of doors, the gas light glistened on moist and empty pavements. Places of amusement closed their doors, and black boards were placed across many windows. Only Queen Victoria was happy. She had gone to join Albert.

Opposite Queen Victoria as she was often seen in old age – gazing lovingly at portraits and mementoes of Prince Albert.

"**Then I shall see another star in the sky.**" *Attributed to a Zulu chief on hearing of the death of "the great White Queen"*

Table of Dates

1819   Birth of Queen Victoria

1825   First passenger railway opened

1832   First Reform Act

1837   Death of William IV; Victoria becomes Queen

1839   Sir Robert Peel resigns as Prime Minister over the "Ladies of the Bedchamber"

1840   Queen Victoria marries Prince Albert of Saxe-Coburg
Birth of the Princess Royal

1841   Peel replaces Lord Melbourne as Prime Minister
Birth of Albert Edward, Prince of Wales

1845   Building of Osborne House on the Isle of Wight begins

1846   Repeal of the Corn Laws

1848   Abdication of Louis Philippe of France
Chartists mass on Kennington Common, London

1851   The Great Exhibition is held in Hyde Park

1852   Lord Aberdeen becomes Prime Minister

1853   Work begins on building Balmoral

1854   Outbreak of Crimean War

1855   Lord Palmerston becomes Prime Minister
Sebastopol captured

1857   Outbreak of the Indian Mutiny

1858   Prince Albert given the title of Prince Consort

1861   Death of the Duchess of Kent, the Queen's mother
Death of Prince Albert

1865   Death of King Leopold of Belgium

1866   Queen Victoria opens Parliament for the first time since the death of her husband

1867   Second Reform Act

1868	Disraeli becomes Prime Minister; is deposed by Gladstone in the same year
1870	Napoleon III is deposed after Franco-Prussian war, and flees to England
1874	Disraeli becomes Prime Minister
1875	Disraeli purchases Khedive of Egypt's shares in the Suez Canal
1877	Queen Victoria proclaimed Empress of India Disraeli becomes Earl of Beaconsfield
1878	Congress of Berlin resolves Russo-Turkish dispute Cyprus ceded to Britain
1880	Gladstone becomes Prime Minister
1881	Death of Disraeli
1884	Third Reform Act
1886	Liberal Party splits over Irish Home Rule
1887	Queen Victoria's Golden Jubilee
1888	Queen Victoria's grandson Willy becomes Kaiser Wilhelm II of Germany
1897	Queen Victoria's Diamond Jubilee
1899	Outbreak of Boer War
1900	Foundation of the Labour Party
1901	Queen Victoria dies at Osborne

Principal Characters

Victoria – Queen of England and Empress of India
Edward, Duke of Kent – fourth son of George III, Queen Victoria's father
Victoria, Duchess of Kent – Queen Victoria's mother
Prince Albert of Saxe-Coburg-Gotha – the Queen's husband, the Prince Consort
Leopold of Saxe-Coburg-Saafield – husband of George IV's daughter; Victoria's uncle, and first King of the Belgians
Baroness Louise Lehzen – a governess who became the Queen's confidante
Baron Stockmar – a doctor who became Prince Albert's adviser
Sir James Clark – the Queen's physician
John Brown – the Queen's Highland servant

Queen Victoria's Children
  Victoria (1840–1901)
  Albert Edward, Prince of Wales, later King Edward VII (1841–1910)
  Alice (1843–1878)
  Alfred, Duke of Edinburgh (1844–1900)
  Helena (1846–1923)
  Louise (1848–1939)
  Arthur, Duke of Connaught (1850–1942)
  Leopold, Duke of Albany (1853–1884)
  Beatrice (1857–1944)

Queen Victoria's Prime Ministers

Lord Melbourne (1835–41)

Sir Robert Peel (1841–46)

Lord John Russell (1846–52; 1865–66)

Lord Derby (1852; 1858–59; 1866–68)

Lord Aberdeen (1852–55)

Lord Palmerston (1855–58; 1859–65)

Benjamin Disraeli (later Lord Beaconsfield) (1868; 1874–80)

W. E. Gladstone (1868–74; 1880–85; 1886; 1892–94)

Lord Salisbury (1885–86; 1896–1901)

Lord Rosebery (1894–96)

Left Grandmother and grandson – the Duchess of Kent with the Prince of Wales in 1858.

Further Reading

There are many hundreds of books about the Victorian Age, of which only a few may be mentioned here. Of those written with secondary school children in mind, two volumes in the WAYLAND DOCUMENTARY HISTORY SERIES are particularly useful: Patrick Rooke's *The Age of Dickens* (Wayland 1970 and *1973) on the social background, and the same author's *Gladstone and Disraeli* (Wayland 1970 and *1973) on the political duel which lasted through much of the reign.

Among general books, the following are just a few of the most interesting and readable:

Cecil, Lord David: *Lord M* (Constable 1965 and *Pan 1969)

Longford, Lady Elizabeth: *Victoria R.I.* (Weidenfeld and Nicolson 1964 and *Pan 1966)

Magnus, Sir Philip: *Gladstone, a Biography* (*John Murray 1954)

Magnus, Sir Philip: *King Edward the Seventh* (John Murray 1964)

Marshall, Dorothy: *The Life and Times of Victoria* (Weidenfeld and Nicolson 1972)

Ridley, Jasper: *Lord Palmerston* (Constable 1970 and *Panther 1972)

Strachey, Lytton: *Eminent Victorians* (Chatto and Windus 1918 and *Penguin 1970)

Strachey, Lytton: *Queen Victoria* (Chatto and Windus 1921 and *Penguin 1970)

Turner, E. S.: *The Court of St. James* (Michael Joseph 1959)

*Paperback edition

Index

The numbers in *italic* type refer to the illustrations.

Picture Credits

The author and publishers wish to thank those who have given permission for the reproduction of copyright illustrations on the following pages: Radio Times Hulton Picture Library, *Frontispiece*, 9, 24, 31, 34, 36, 41, 44 *bottom*, 46, 47, 48, 55, 69, 80, 82, 84 *bottom*, 85, 89, 93; Mary Evans Picture Library, 6, 12, 16, 18, 23, 26, 59; The Mansell Collection, 20, 28, 33, 52, 68 *right, jacket back*; *Queen* magazine, 62; City of London Corporation, *jacket front*. Pictures on the following pages are the property of the Wayland Picture Library: 8, 10, 13, 14, 15, 21, 25, 30, 35, 37, 38, 40, 44 *top*, 45, 54, 56, 58, 60, 65, 66, 68 *left*, 70, 71, 73, 74, 76, 79, 83, 84 *top*, 87.